Unlocking Capital: A Guide for Entrepreneurs

RG KASHYAP

CONTENTS

Chapter 1

WHAT YOU SHOULD KNOW ABOUT ATTRACTING MONEY

It is an odd phenomenon that people who have the courage to start a business are often unaware of their ability to attract a wide range of financial possibilities. This is an exceptional phenomenon since it is rare for individuals to have the bravery to start a company. This is an odd event simply because it is a strange occurrence. And I'm not talking about the exorbitant bank fees you had to pay years ago.

If you are the owner or CEO of a company, please accept my congratulations! I cannot describe how pleased I am that you are interested in this. If you read this book, follow the advice in it, and put it into practise, you have a high chance of being paid for having the courage (some may even say insanity) to turn your original concept into a viable company. You may do this by following the suggestions in this book. Your company's present status is probably more akin to a young sapling, but it's also possible that it's a fully grown oak. Do you feel that a plant of any size needs a consistent and continuous supply of water in order to survive? If so, what is your stance on the subject? To maintain their existing rates of growth, all types of businesses need a steady supply of new financial resources.

Does it occur to you that it is now astonishingly feasible for businesses to attract investors in almost any circumstance? This rule has just a few exceptions. My personal interest in private equity was spurred by the shocking realisation that some firms grow simply because they know how to get cash, rather than because of better strategy, more motivated workers, or leaner operating methods. This realisation ignited my interest in private equity. This eye-opening realisation sparked my interest in the field of private equity as a career option. It all boils down to understanding the various funding options and how to get them.

My parents started a typesetting business when they were in their mid-fifties, despite the fact that neither of them had any prior experience in the field. At that point in their life, this was an exceedingly fresh thing for them to do. Even more remarkable is the fact that they have managed to retain a reasonable level of living over the previous half-century. They excelled in a wide range of activities and had a clear vision of where they wanted to go and how to deal with the quickly changing technological environment. Others, on the other hand, lacked grasp of a certain aspect of financial problems. They failed to see that there were other options for financing their firm and that a significant number of prospective investors would have given everything to work with them. They also overlooked the fact that a sizable number of prospective investors would have given everything to collaborate with them.

They also ran the most desirable kind of business, one with expensive equipment that could be sold in order to return creditors' money. The bank saw that things had changed for the better. It made ridiculous amounts of money available to be returned in numerous ways, but it didn't provide much in the way of strategic assistance. Despite the fact that they lacked the necessary abilities, my parents intended to grow their firm to the point where it could support more than simply their living expenses. They would have been able to succeed with their company if they had more financial resources and more boardroom expertise.

Outsiders with Talent

My parents were afraid to confront money; therefore, they did not make the necessary purchases, did not invest in new product lines, and did not buy the necessary equipment. This generated several issues for the family. Since they didn't understand the idea, they assumed that no one would be interested in investing as a partner. This was despite the fact that they had regular cash flows and fantastic client contracts. Even though it would have benefited them to be more aware of trends and competition, my parents were unfamiliar with the concept of private equity. Despite the fact that my parents were completely unaware of the notion, they did not read any books or attend any conferences since they were unaware that other organizations provided financial help as well. This was not due to a lack of time; rather, they were ignorant that other organizations provided financial assistance. They assumed that the only two options for obtaining financing were the stock market and the bank. When it came time to sell the business after a long and tough trip, the new owner was the one who enjoyed the fruits of my parents' laborious labor and made the most of the opportunities that emerged because of their efforts. After spending the previous 15 years coaching educated and driven businesses on strategy, I saw that in order for my parents' outstanding ideas to succeed, they needed funding from outside sources. I was able to do so since I had spent the previous 15 years counseling executives on company strategy. Along the same lines as my parents, I assumed that the only ways to get money were via the issuance of stocks on the open market or through the use of financial institutions. Given that I am now aware that this is not the case, I wrote this book to serve as a resource for all entrepreneurs, regardless of where they are in the process of launching their business, whether they are considering an initial public offering (IPO), planning to sell their business for a profit, or doing one of these things for the first time. I wrote this book as a reference for all entrepreneurs, whether they are pursuing an IPO, preparing to sell their firm for a profit, or just starting out. Since everything is part of the trip, understanding what lies ahead allows you to go more rapidly. It is important to remember that the quantity of money you earn does not matter, whether it is $30,000, $5,000,000, or $50,000,000, and it is critical to remember that this does not matter. It is critical to call attention to this specific reality. Private equity financing in the millions of dollars is available, and investors are looking for successful enterprises owned and controlled by astute business owners. Even if you feel your firm isn't very good — possibly because it's too tiny, doesn't generate enough income, or has too few workers — you could be shocked at how much respect others have for it. Even if you assume your firm isn't very excellent, this might be the case. I can say this because, in my experience, the kind of organizations that investors prefer and want — yes, even those that are not yet successful — have frequently astounded me. That's why I'm able to say it. This is something I can say with assurance because of my previous experiences.

McGregor Socks, a well-known Canadian company, is a wonderful illustration of this. They've been in business for quite some time. As a consequence of having difficulty responding to the quickly changing conditions of the global market, McGregor concluded that the firm needed to build a market in China for the knitted works of Canadian design that it produced. The money was donated by a private equity company because the fund's investors had past experience conducting business in China and thought that doing so would benefit the fund. Even if the transition to partnering is difficult, a wonderful Canadian brand (check for a pair of McGregor's socks the next time you need socks) remains on store shelves because of the support of investors.

What Is Private Equity?

The term "private equity" refers to monies that are maintained privately and then invested in privately owned businesses that are not publicly traded. These businesses lack access to public marketplaces. Investments may occasionally include large sums of money, such as the one million dollars that your uncle Jim gave to the video game company that your brother owns and manages. No one will be able to buy or sell shares in it since it is not publicly traded and is not listed anywhere, so that option is ruled out. Yet, this definition does not account for the significant distinctions that might exist between private equity and other kinds of capital. David Rubenstein of The Carlyle Group, generally regarded as one of the most renowned figures in the world of private equity, gets straight to the point. "Investments made by persons who already own a part of a business are referred to as private equity," and "private equity" is an umbrella word for various sorts of investments. These individuals will put money into the firm, work to help it grow and improve, and then sell their ownership holdings in the company. Moreover, the idea of "private equity" may be divided into three distinct subcategories: "what," "how," and "result."

The What

When a firm obtains private equity funding, it receives a percentage of the company's ownership as well as a longer amount of time than is customary for a bank loan to put the money to use in order to expand the business. Private equity is a sort of investment. When seeking to define private equity, one of the most frequent methods to do so is to refer to the total amount of money invested in the firm. Your company's current stage of development will determine not just the quantity of private equity investment funds that you need but also the kind of investor that you should seek. A "venture capitalist," for example, would usually only invest in a company if it needed more than $2 million in financing. This is due to venture investors' desire for big returns on their investments. To put it another way, your firm's maturity level will determine not only the sorts of private equity investors interested in your business but also the amount of money they are willing to spend   on   it.
According to Rick Nathan, president of the Canadian Venture Capital Association (CVCA) and partner at Kensington Capital, it is difficult to agree on a definition that is understood by all stakeholders engaged in the financial business. Rick Nathan made one of these comments. Nathan and I both agree on this topic. For example, some people think that a firm must have yearly sales of at least $50 million in order to access private equity, while others

UNLOCKING CAPITAL: A GUIDE FOR ENTREPRENEURS

believe that private equity may be obtained from "angels" or individuals who spend less than $1 million. These two schools of thought are both wrong. According to Nathan, the term "private equity" may apply to a wide variety of unique economic operations, including top-tier buyouts, institutional funds, venture capital, angel investors, and seed funding for brand new enterprises. To put it another way, all of the funds remain in private hands and are invested in companies actively seeking fresh sources of cash.

The How

Consider a private equity investor to be like a good baseball coach, encouraging and guiding you as you throw and catch the ball at a much higher level than you have previously been able to achieve. This coach will assist you in throwing and catching the ball at a much higher level than you have previously been able to achieve. This coach will help you get to the next level of your game. The "how" of investing in private equity is not standardized since each transaction has its own negotiation procedure to define the terms and parameters of the deal. These qualities include the board's engagement as well as how the communication and decision-making processes will work in the future. A private equity investor will often, but not always, purchase an equity stake in the company directly from the corporation. Yet, this is not always the case. When it comes to taking action and making decisions, the Board of Directors may do so on a variety of levels. Private equity investors are motivated to continue working towards the firm's success since they participate in both the risks and the rewards of their relationship with the business. When the transaction is completed and the funds are transferred, the private equity investor will try to enhance the corporation's overall effectiveness in order to maximize the return on their investment, in a manner similar to that of a sports coach. They will do this by using a more active and dynamic management strategy, which will also assist transformation in organizations that have been in operation for a longer period of time. You, as the founder or current owner of the

14

firm, will discover that an effective strategy for the company's development, expansion, or resuscitation may be advantageous.

The Result

The third and final component of the private equity idea is known as the huge zinger, bringing the total number of components to three. Private equity is commonly referred to as "patient capital" since it pays out money over a long period of time, generally three to six years. Due to the way your business partners work with the rest of your team, there's a strong possibility you'll be able to go farther in the major leagues than you previously imagined was possible. Private equity investors are encouraged to build it since they are investing in your company rather than just giving you money at a set rate of return. This makes private equity a more appealing investment option. After five years, they will signal that they want to sell their stake in the business and will offer you, your group, a larger company, or the broader public the opportunity to buy their shares. The investor will ask you in all seriousness what you dare to dream of in five years; consequently, you should prepare your response to this question before the meeting. For the sake of simplicity, we shall combine the startup stages of venture capital (starting at $1 million and going up), private equity (beginning at $10 million and continuing up), and angel money (beginning at $100,000 and going up) under the name "private equity." This will include all three kinds of investments. The phrase "buyout" will not be used. For example, Ford's big acquisitions of Hertz are the darlings of business journalists because they shift ownership of the organization away from the public stock market and into private funding. Notwithstanding the fact that the $1 billion sale of a publicly listed firm, Domino's Pizza, to a private equity group headed by Bain Capital is beyond the scope of this book owing to the size of the private equity sector, we will analyze the techniques that contributed to their success. As can be seen, private equity investors are referred to using a number of different terms, each of which represents the amount of money that they are putting into the endeavor. For the sake of simplicity, we will refer to all of these partners as "fund managers" or "the investor," rather than "angel investors," "venture capitalists (often branded "VCs")," and the more formal phrase "institutional fund manager." This is because each of these partners is in charge of managing the firm's finances and investing in them. Nevertheless, if the process of seeking investments is sufficiently similar for this book, each stakeholder will be analyzed individually since the reasons private equity and venture capital investors make their investments are rather different. As a result, the search of investment possibilities will be treated as a single problem. You've undoubtedly heard of Research in Motion (RIM), Open Text, Porter Airlines, Sleiman, Sleep Country mattresses, and Upper Canada beer. As seen by their expansion, private equity investors were critical to the success of each of these businesses. Then there are the unnoticed economic players, such as Valtrex, which for in multimedia; Bridgeport, which develops mobile phone technology; Spintex, which manufactures yarn; Birmingham, which manufactures construction equipment; or even businesses that shred paper, manufacture parts for the automotive industry, supply nursing homes with supplies, and so on and so forth. Every one of these companies will say that private equity helped their operations in some way, and this will be accurate. A firm owner who is familiar with the industry and an investor who has prior experience may be able to build something that is greater than what either of them could have achieved on their own. They can build a thriving firm that explodes like spectacular pyrotechnics, revealing landscapes that are far from their comfy garden.

Money for All Sizes

The first piece of hopeful news is that private equity is accessible to a wide variety of enterprises, not simply those with the potential to be sold publicly. This difference is significant since it implies that more firms will be able to benefit from private equity. Private investors are prepared to consider contributing money to enterprises that need as little as a half-million dollars, as much as ten billion dollars, or even as much as one hundred billion dollars for new projects. The amount of money required by these enterprises might vary from zero to one hundred billion dollars. If specific requirements are met, private investors may consider investing in firms with needs as little as $500,000. This is a comprehensive book in and of itself. You must realize that at the end of this book, you will be able to recognize the many distinct sorts of investors associated with each level. This is something you should be aware of. This is something you should be aware of. People are realizing that the current situation is out of the ordinary, and the number of people who have reached this conclusion is growing. Those who succeed in business are the new kind of heroes. According to Industry Canada statistics, 2.3 million small and medium-sized enterprises (SMEs) employ 65% of all workers in the Canadian economy. Even while the time has come for state governments to go above and beyond in their support of entrepreneurial initiatives, individuals aren't simply sitting around doing nothing. Young people with ambition often attend seminars to learn how to succeed on their own, without the support of an uncle who works in the field. For example, the operations of new company owners are becoming more complex, and these owners are realizing that there are different ways to collect money in addition to the traditional ones. In other words, the activities of new company owners are becoming more complex. As if business owners didn't have enough on their plates already, they're being encouraged to take their abilities seriously and enroll in university courses like "entrepreneurship and creating money." As if they didn't have enough on their plates already. In addition to organizing competitions for the finest business proposals, business schools provide a plethora of entrepreneurship-focused courses. The winners of these competitions get $40,000 in start-up funds to apply towards the growth of their firm. These are all little smoke signals that, when combined, provide the message that actual company owners, whether they operate industrial enterprises that have been in operation for a century or brand-new startups, can make a lot of money. This is true whether they are running manufacturing organizations that have been in existence for a hundred years or brand-new startups. There is a brand-new, high-end dining table available for CEOs and business owners of small to mid-sized firms, equipped with an enticing array of methods to attract money to your company (as well as your retirement funds), so that you and your spouse may live the lifestyle you both want. The fundamental premise behind this work is that a brand new, high-end dining table is now accessible for chief executive officers and company owners of small to medium-sized businesses.

Private Equity Is One Arrow in Your Bow

There are several methods to get financial support, including low- or high-leveraged bank loans, private money, and the open market. Another source of monetary resources is the free market. Even though we will concentrate on private equity, you should be aware that you have access to a wide variety of alternative options. For example, depending on the specifics of your situation, the public market or a bank may be a better alternative for you to explore. There is a chance that the variety may cause some confusion at times. The table is in the center of the image. It gives a short summary of the many sources of money, which is quite useful. One step at a time, things are getting clearer. There is an increasing availability of financial resources that firms may utilize. It is the most efficient method for the loan practice. Since there have never been so many financial prospects open to previously devalued parts of a firm, a good proportion of business owners have reason to be positive about the future. This is due to previously undervalued components of the organization becoming more valuable in recent years. Most business owners believe that private equity is only used for large corporate takeovers, such as KKR's historic acquisition of RJR Nabisco, or based on extensive press coverage of Teacher's Pension Funds, Torstar, and Woodbridge's offer to purchase BCE stock, which has a potential value of 1.8 billion dollars. Private equity, on the other hand, is employed for much more than just massive business takeovers. Ford, Dunkin' Donuts, Domino's, Hertz, and Toys-R-Us, among others, are often included in the headlines of news on private equity purchases of Fortune 500 companies. Private equity, on the other hand, may be utilized for smaller purchases, such as Woodbridge's attempt to buy a minority ownership in the companies Ford, Dunkin' Donuts, Domino's, and Hertz, among others. Even if these deals are available, you may not be able to take advantage of them. Since

2001, the private equity industry has grown at an unprecedented rate; yet, this expansion is due to more than simply the deals that generate headlines.
According to Ed Reclean, a former partner at Uncap, one of Canada's leading private equity firms—Jerry Schwartz's Onex—these billion-dollar acquisitions account for around 1% of all private equity agreements overall, as assessed by the number of deals executed rather than the cash amount. Jerry Schwartz's Onex offered this information. Ed Reclean worked for Onex when it was recognized as Canada's premier private equity firm. According to the findings of a survey conducted by McKinsey & Company in 2006 and titled "Private Equity Canada," the most lucrative opportunities for private equity can be found in Canada among the hundreds of privately owned small businesses that are currently undergoing competitive and succession transitions. Despite the fact that the great majority of transactions take place in the small to medium-sized market, these transactions are seldom mentioned on the front page. What precisely is the allure of owning a trucking company with a $10 million yearly income, respectable compensation for the CEO, and the largest luxury being the purchase of warehouses to expand supply chain knowledge? 2
The good news for you as an entrepreneur is that when you look at what falls under the category of private capital, it becomes as plain as the nose on your face that huge transactions account for a very tiny fraction of the bulk of opportunities available for firms like yours to pursue. This is fantastic news since it implies that the majority of the agreements available for firms like yours to pursue do not entail significant sums of money. This is because negotiating conditions for large transactions is generally more complex and time-consuming than negotiating terms for smaller ones.

Traditional Finance May Follow the Record Industry

Traditional methods of funding, such as the lending ratios and tables at the local bank, as well as the limits and expectations for quarterly results imposed by public stock markets, might prove to be burdensome for a small firm that is in the process of growing. In the world of finance, an era that was characterized by honey-colored full harvest moons and gentle winds that carried the scent of summer hay into the atmosphere is soon coming to an end. A whiff of winter can now be detected in the air for the very first time.

However, financing sources for smaller, riskier businesses are quickly expanding as more inexperienced participants, such as firm owners who cashed out at the peak of the IT boom, infuse funds into the market. This growth is being driven by inexperienced participants who cashed out at the peak of the IT boom. Many who sold their companies during the peak of the information technology boom are among the new participants. These investors are working to find more adaptable methods of compensating entrepreneurs, including people such as yourself who are willing to take the risk of launching businesses. In addition, these tactics will be used to compensate larger institutional funds that were established with capital pools provided by outside investors. They are also allowed to participate in more risky areas, such as the software industry, which traditional financial institutions are not permitted to enter because doing so would put the assets of their customers at unacceptable risk of loss. However, these companies are allowed to participate in the software industry. Banks are willing to finance ventures even if it means taking on a lesser proportion of the total risk and selling off a portion of the loan to private equity investors. This is because private equity investors are willing to take on more risk in exchange for higher returns. Imagine a time around one billion years ago when the whole surface of the planet was a single mass referred to as Pangaea and was surrounded by the salty waters of the Panthalassa Sea. This can help you gain a better understanding of the changes that are now taking place. When something happened, an eruption of a volcano functioned as the trigger event, and the land started to separate into irregularly shaped lumps. Through time, these lumps of land ultimately became the diverse land masses that make up the continents that we know today. It is difficult to fathom how something that, on the surface, seems to be unchangeable might have, in the past, morphed into something that was completely unexpected and incomprehensible.

Something quite similar has taken place in the traditional business model of the banking industry. This tendency gained steam with the widespread availability of personal computers and the Internet. In the same way that technological advancements have rendered conventional methods of funding ineffective, the use of typewriters as a means of getting one's ideas down on paper is now considered antiquated. The term "private equity" refers to irrationally proportioned pieces of private wealth that are fast distancing themselves from the majority of public capital pools. This process is occurring very quickly. This process is analogous to the gradual disintegration of Pangaea, which was followed by the formation of an entirely new planet. It is possible to establish these funds, which are comprised of groups of professionals in a certain area and use them to make investments in businesses that will profit from the skill set that the specialists bring to the table. They are able to do so as a result of technological advancements, which enable them to assess daily performance while also having access to spreadsheets and the capability to delve deeply into financial spreadsheets. Because of this, they can achieve all of their goals. Even as recently as 20 years ago, information of this kind on the company's financial situation was not accessible. Researching businesses, executives, and customers can now be done in a timely and comprehensive manner because of the proliferation of the Internet. Because of this, the money that is available to invest in businesses like yours will be carefully analyzed, problems will be resolved quickly, and performance will be managed in a more effective manner, all of which will lead to increased financial returns for everyone involved.

To tell you the truth, "quantities" are the primary factor responsible for the recent decline in the state of the public markets. The anticipation among shareholders of rising quarterly profits dampens the joy that comes with the development of a company, due to the fact that each new endeavor will have a deleterious effect on those earnings. An absentee investor who demands that the business dole out cash and runs the firm like an ATM is wasting the money that was provided by taxpayers. This investor also treats the company like an ATM. The public stances of shareholders are something that chief executives are strongly

encouraged   to   avoid.
Private equity investments are made in the business in a way that
the public market does not, in contrast to public money
investments, which enable companies to become public but are
subsequently likely to be forgotten by investors. This is because
private equity investors are ready to take on the long-term risk that
comes with investing in intangible assets such as research and
development and innovation. This is why we have this situation.
You may have noticed that the music industry is breaking apart,
despite the best efforts of the big players to shore up the crumbling
walls. Despite their best efforts, the falling walls are getting worse.
The music industry is analogous to the Tower of Pisa, with the
exception that it is falling apart at a somewhat faster rate. They go
to extreme lengths, such as bringing lawsuits against their main
demographic, teens, for unlawfully downloading music, to control
the antiquated economic model so that it may be used indefinitely.
One example of this is when they sue teenagers for downloading
music illegally. Please put some thought into what you're filming,
men. The endeavor is at an end. Even though the traditional music
industry has been one of the most lucrative victims of the digital
era, public financial markets such as the Dow Jones have realized
that technology is changing the rules of the game for them as well.
Technology advancements have made it possible for music lovers
to acquire their preferred tracks in a variety of different ways.
Some of these methods include downloading songs directly from
rock bands, purchasing albums from independent record labels, or
purchasing a single hit song through Apple's iTunes. You don't
have to buy the whole album of terrible B-sides just to get your
hands on that one hit song; you can acquire it from a single
download. In a similar vein, the initial public offering (IPO) is no
longer the be-all and end-all for entrepreneurs who are eager to
grow their businesses. Now, there are one hundred different funds
available for company owners to borrow money from in order to
finance   their   companies.
As business owners realize that it is not necessary for their
companies to be publicly traded on a stock exchange in order to
have access to capital, older ways of thinking are beginning to
catch up with the new geography of money.

Challenges Facing CEOs and Owners

Before delving into the mechanics of private capital, also known as private equity, it is critical to understand why the stock market is no longer the primary source of funding. Since the stock market is no longer the major source of finance, this is the situation. To begin, excessive regulation is being imposed on publicly traded firms as the government attempts to calm the outcry produced by a small number of rotten apples (Enron) that harmed the whole stock market. Businesses are the ones who end up footing the bill as they cope with the costs of conforming to ever-tighter rules and regulations devised by bureaucrats. This is because firms must bear the price of adhering to ever-tighter laws and regulations. The stock market on Wall Street is influenced by legislation such as Sarbanes-Oxley, which may be seen positively. Public corporations are drowning in a sea of paperwork, devoting time, money, and energy to completing reports demonstrating that they are not laundering money for terrorists or embezzling money via the compensation committee. These studies show that public corporations are not involved in unlawful actions. As a result, market forces are clamoring for a better way of doing things since public firms spend time, money, and energy producing reports that show they are not embezzling money via the pay committee. This is due to the need for public corporations to report on their financial activity. Concerned about the firm's steadily declining profitability, board members arrive with their own legal counsel and a determination to bear as little risk in the organization's management as is humanly possible. The time spent by management on staying ahead of the competition is no longer accessible. Just in the previous four years, the New York Stock Exchange has lost a market share comparable to 80% of the whole market for global equity offerings. Stephen Schwarzman, a Blackstone Group employee, believes that this will motivate someone to take action and increase the attraction of the public market. Both the Alternative Investment Market (AIM) in the United Kingdom and the Toronto Stock Exchange (TSX) in Canada have yet to face a level of complexity like this. The sector's current paradigm is also criticized for the short-term focus on public stock markets, which is another criticism leveled against it. Every quarter, CEOs are put under great pressure to grow their companies' sales, even though doing so is never in the best interests of the company's long-term value. Nobody can offer excuses or argue, "How could we have known that the markets would not fully invest in new projects or R&D as a consequence of this quarterly whine for growing revenues?" No one knows the solution to that question. Therefore, no one can make excuses or argue, "How could we have known that the markets would not fully invest in new projects or R&D as a consequence of this quarterly braggadocio?" When the common exam question for MBA finance professors was "For 30% of your marks, describe how a CEO may increase the shares of their publicly traded company," warning signs began to appear more than 10 years ago. This was part of the assessment that we had to complete. This was an excellent experiment that demonstrated how a company may get too concerned with quarterly performance. There is a limit to how many times the wine may be diluted before it becomes unfit to drink. The issue is that this often-requested question, which was originally intended to educate students on how to identify a firm whose assets are being liquidated, has now evolved into a legitimate demand from stock market participants. This makes it difficult to teach pupils how to recognize a firm whose assets are being   liquidated.

They have power over the organizations they control since they are shareholders   and   owners   of   public   enterprises. Who else, except the CEO, is accountable for this? If you show the terrible CEOs a public shareholder who is willing to wait for a long-term R&D strategy to take effect while the balance sheet is flat, they will be stunned and gasp for breath. Shareholders demonstrated that they had the attention span of a kindergarten class when the ice cream truck passed by. They also demonstrated that they would dash off to the next desired chance as rapidly as their frail legs would allow. For many years, Warren Buffett's strategy at Berkshire Hathaway Inc. has been diametrically opposed to Wall Street's approach. Buffett invests for the long run and keeps his investments open. This is an intriguing and unusual strategy to take. Who could have foreseen that in their right mind? With its stringent quarterly concentration, the public markets, which had hitherto enjoyed a monopoly on efficient capital, were finally obliged to pay the price for the disturbing popularity of these short-term investment approaches. In other words, they were obliged to pay the price due to the rigid quarterly emphasis on short-term investment tactics. It has been shown that the returns obtained by these procedures outperform those provided by longer-term strategies.

New Ways to Add Value

Wall Street and Bay Street have the same goal: to amass financial resources for the benefit of commercial innovation. It has been successful in achieving its aim for many decades and has done an excellent job throughout that period. But a new component has been introduced to the equation: the growth of the private equity market.

Banks are no longer the sole members of the guild that controls the financial lending market. As a result of the ripple effect, the market has discovered a new way to become more efficient. The ripple effect is responsible for this finding. Farewell, disinterested shareholders whose sole concern was whether the company was being handled in such a manner that dividends could be paid today. Nowadays, private equity teams are endowed with expertise and a global network, and their main question is, "How can we operate with a long-term horizon?" How can we, the management team, and the current owners, collaborate to expand the firm, and what are some of the methods we might use to do so? "In the past, private equity companies had a proclivity to be very deal focused: the bulk of their performance hinged on the identification and execution of deals," according to a KPMG study titled Creating Private Equity Value. Yet, in today's environment, the focus has shifted to the process of creating value and improving performance within the framework of existing assets. The primary purpose of the private equity business is "to add value to a transaction that is in excess of the historical returns," which can be read in their mission statement. 3 Who can blame businesses for ditching an ineffective old business strategy in favor of a more profitable new one? You may be wondering how this money is used for private equity investments. What has been the most recent development? Is it more expensive? Where precisely will you be able to get your hands on some?

The Big Difference Private Equity Brings

According to KPMG, important participants in the global private equity industry have one thing in common: they employ their expertise inside the organisations for which they work. This is one of the qualities that distinguishes these people. Those who have moved cash out of their own businesses and are now actively engaged in the private equity market are the most successful. In the private equity industry, these people have a far higher chance of generating a profit. They can empathise with your predicament. They may stroll through the dirt of an unfamiliar field and instantly comprehend the quantity of blood and sweat required to achieve that degree of sweetness and moisture. This might happen if they are exposed to a variety of situations. They have created a favourable climate for the expansion of their own firm by securing bank loans and finance. They have been blessed with a bountiful harvest after surviving the years needed to germinate and generate a lucrative crop, overcoming the emotional losses caused by hailstorms, and enduring the years required to germinate and establish a successful crop. They are not affected by the condition known as "Qu arteritis" because they understand that seeds cannot be expected to produce green fields in the next quarter. This understanding shields them from the condition's consequences. They like how things have evolved organically in the organisation. They understand the parameters that must be fulfilled for seeds and young plants to mature fully.

They have a healthy respect for the work that went into developing your company and are grateful for it. Abatis is a high-tech company founded in Vancouver by John Seminarian, a graduate of the University of Waterloo's School of Engineering. Seminarian is a Waterloo native. He entered business with the private equity firm Celtic House and formed a relationship with them to raise startup money. The seminar was able to achieve even greater success after the sale of Abatis for more than $2 billion. Seminarian is adding his extraordinary leadership talents to the advancement of the high-tech sector of the economy by participating in the Yaletown and Magellan Angel Partners funds now that he has established a footing in the venture capital business. This is accomplished by his participation in the funds.

Consider the possibility of receiving personalised attention from an entrepreneur who has regularly reached such a high level of success. At this time, it should be plainly clear to you that private equity can do much more for you than just give financial support. It is conceivable that with the help of private equity, you will be able to increase your revenues to a greater extent than you could on your own or with the help of a bank loan. The desire of private equity firms wants your company to thrive and provide them with a return on their investment as well as extra earnings that will have an impact on your business. As a result of this, your organization will profit in the long run. They also benefit from the improved performance of their incentives. They treat the quest for the same profits at the end of the game with the same seriousness as the owner does. This mental adjustment in one's financial circumstances is not only revolutionary; it is a necessary transformation in and of itself. It's a thrilling experience that's also dangerous. It is by far the most amazing inducement available in the private equity market. This is a real partnership in which both parties benefit from the connection.

Lender and Owner

It's likely that you'll find yourself wondering why you need private equity investors if the bank can take care of everything for you. When you lend money to individuals at a lower interest rate, your business will be doing rather well for itself. Why would you put yourself in danger by doing that? It would be necessary for me to sell part of the shares that represent a portion of the ownership position I hold in my firm, is that correct? Is it really in your best interest to give up significant stock for the benefit of a partner that you don't know anything about? To answer your question in a nutshell, you can. In the same way that money is held by investors in banks and public markets, much of the money in private equity is owned by investors. Funds are managed by financial experts, business professionals, or wealthy people who have achieved success in their careers or businesses. The key distinction is that these investors want to have a hands-on role in the project that they are funding. This is something that quite a few property owners consider to be an excessive source of anxiety. They have a mental image of an opposing army invading their place of business, replete with the sound of clacking Armor and shuffling boots. Armor ringing throughout their workplaces and factories as their employees huddle in the darkness behind their desks, trembling with terror and hoping that these newcomers will be welcomed. Treat one another with respect, and do not open fire on anybody. It will be more enjoyable for a chief executive officer to oversee a company that has the necessary capital to complete the overarching goal as well as a savvy private equity team that brings capabilities to the company. These capabilities could include assisting in the recruitment of that CFO or organizing a trip to China through reputable and reliable contacts. Some private equity firms generate higher profits by using leverage on their balance sheets and engaging in other dubious financial methods to achieve their objectives. Robert Posen, an employee of MFS Investment Management, regularly refers to the study conducted by McKinsey. According to the findings of the research that was carried out, most private equity purchases that were evaluated focused their attention on the "main driver of value creation in the company's performance rather than its financial leverage." Our natural reluctance to relinquish possession is a sentiment that is quite comprehensible. Pertaining to a person who owns a company Having said that, there is no rule that says the ownership must be permanent. You have the option of acquiring your prior company while simultaneously building up your stake in it. A period will eventually come to an end. Please give it one more go before giving up in despair and giving up on reading before it's too late. Private equity is given a decent amount of attention. Get information about the participants and the needs they have. and, most importantly, the primary motivations behind their actions. They do it because they share your degree of interest in and obsession with business. This is the reason why they do it.

The Benefit of Private Equity

"The winner of the media category is Ernst & Young Entrepreneur of the Year—Somerset Entertainment!" exclaimed the speaker. Somerset Entertainment was named the winner of the award. Andy Burgess came up onto the podium to claim the trophy with a brilliant grin on his face. This moment of joy came after many years of working till late at night to attain what may have seemed to be an easy accomplishment—standing there in a tuxedo, waving the trophy. Andy Burgess is one of the owners of Somerset Entertainment, which develops and distributes specialized music to gift shops and other non-traditional stores using interactive displays that enable consumers to listen to CDs by pushing a button. These displays are seen at gift shops. The eyes now have 28,000 displays at around 18,500 venues, which include both general merchandisers and businesses that specialize in a certain profession.

Somerset Entertainment made a lot of purchases in order to grow their firm and load their shelves with Juno awards, and they moved from $5 million in sales to $11 million in revenues. They eventually made $21 million in income. After the purchase of a distributor in 1998, the eye leveraged its assets by incurring four forms of debt: term debt, debt with a 17% interest rate, revolving credit, and a vendor takeback loan. At this moment, the first hints of failure appeared. When Andy inquired, "Can you manage a larger volume?" The Buff-A-Loo distribution and fulfilment center had been delivering to over a hundred different retail locations with success. They automatically replied, "Yes!" even though this was far from the case. Somerset was a corporation with $8 million in sales and $2 million in EBITDA before growing into the supply chain approach (profits before interest, tax, depreciation, and amortization; see glossary for definition). Unfortunately, the firm had grown into this manner with a distributor who was habitually late and had an uncanny ability to botch up orders. The eye would say that they had shipped products, which turned out to be the CD display case. Somerset would then charge the retailer, which, as it turned out, had only received a bill. It was October, the biggest selling month before the holidays, and Christmas was just around the corner. That's not good! The American merchant class is renowned for being tenacious, and they were furious when they discovered they had been misled. The eye told Andy that they had not been successful in obtaining the materials and then convinced him that he did not need to come over any longer since they had completed their objective. Yikes! Somerset had gone from being lightning-fast at delivering orders to being slow and unreliable in a single rapid move. "We topped $36 million in sales with $8.5 million in EBITDA, but our debt was at $15 million, and for the balance of the term, we agonized over breaking covenants." After getting a valuation of $15 million, we decided, if reluctantly, to accept a private equity investment of $21 million Looking back, Andy feels that obtaining private equity was an excellent move for the owners' motivation, since it removed some of the stress connected with worries about money and retirement. We were able to instantly split a sizable chunk of the business for ourselves while maintaining complete control since private equity companies bought a portion of our company's ownership." I had worked hard, and it felt amazing to be able to present the company's founder and owners with $6 million. Somerset was able to pay off its debts immediately and still maintain a $4 million cash reserve for future acquisitions thanks to this money. "With that extra money," Andy continues, "we built up an off-cue in Chicago that has proved to be the crucial catapult into the American market, taking Somerset to the next level." Even though we had a difficult year at the firm, there was no reason for us to be anxious about its demise. We were finally able to unwind and focus on preparing for the approaching storm and devising a new plan for going forward therefore. Somerset's private equity partners were useful sounding boards as the company sought to grow via acquisitions. Although they had a more aggressive aim for expansion, the investors backed Somerset's decision to abandon specific targets. "Moreover, when we were about to lose a critical worker, the investors did bring him around and persuade him to stay," Andy says. "The investors drew him in and convinced him to remain." "When you are an entrepreneur working your tail off, it is great to have that cash distribution in addition to having finances to build the firm," Andy says. When you invest in private equity, you have the financial liquidity you need without the public market's scrutiny. To put it another way, you get the best of both worlds. According to Andy, going public is not an option for many firms. "You'll get through this shift with private equity." Check to verify whether you are allowed to go public. Please complete Andy's exam and make sure the relevant checkmarks are next to your chart. You generate enough money to meet the expenses of public listing and accounting.

You have a decent profit table. Your sales have a solid growth curve. You have competent management staff. You have a good build. "At the time of the private equity acquisition, we were too small to go public," Andy is quoted as saying. We were able to retain ownership of the firm while expanding cash owed to private equity investors. We were on the verge of bankruptcy owing to risky debt, but private equity rescued us just in time. Before 2005, when Somerset did our first public offense, eyes were the steppingstone to getting big enough. Selling the secondary shares was also a terrific experience. Andy Burgess had an epiphany as he stood on stage, allowing the audience's adulation to wash over him. He realized how far Somerset Entertainment had progressed and how amazing the adventure had been up to that moment.

Your Competitors Will Get Private Money

Make no doubt about it. Be aware of the person competing against you. It is critical that you keep up with the Joneses. In addition, the private equity market will be scrutinized. It's probable that the eye has already begun discussions with potential equity partners. What would be the most damaging thing they could do to your firm if they suddenly had a million dollars? What would the Jones family be able to achieve with merely $5 million if your yearly income was roughly $6 million? Did you say there was a lot of damage? What if the Joneses' new best friend was John Seminarian, who was previously touted as an expert in your sector with a larger view of the worldwide market? Assume for a minute that the Jones family had access to the skilled help required to manage the large supply chain that begins in China and to shift the bulk of manufacturing to Mr. Private Equity's well-established ties in Shanghai. What if, like the profit table at Cineplex Galaxy, Jerry Schwartz, the CEO of Onex and one of the leading lights in private equity, attended their board meetings and opened his Rolodex? How have you found your previous encounters with private equity? By the way, equity investors will love you if your company can't possibly move production to China because you're in the service or transportation industries, or because your products are too heavy or bulky to be economically floated across the Pacific because it would be difficult for your company to be destroyed by cheaper imports. This is due to the difficulty of economically floating your firm over the Pacific.

It is the Baby Boomers Again

All of this is subject to one important proviso. Finally, the python that is processing that enormous mass known as the Baby Boomers is coming closer and closer to the finish line of its meal. The Baby Boomer generation is now entering their senior years. This indicates that they are already in the process of selling their companies, a process that will pick up speed over the following fifty years as they approach the age when they can spend their days relaxing on the porch. The private financing market will be distorted by the Baby Boomer life cycle, just as it has been in every market that came before it. These prosperous days for private equity will come to an end since a significant amount of money comes from shifting business patterns. That is as predictable as a summer blockbuster movie made in Hollywood. In the same way that Holland experienced tulip mania in the 17th century or the dot-com bubble in the year 2000, the current economic climate is seeing a boom in private equity. While you are in the thick of things, it might be difficult to keep in mind that everything will ultimately "pop." Increasing the size of your business, sometimes known as "scaling up," makes it more appealing to private equity investors. You need to get started right away if you are serious about luring investors to your company. The chance for company owners and chief executive officers to have access to investment capital has never been greater than it is right now. Throughout the next five years, there will be significant shifts in the new financial possibilities. Riding the wave of private investment is the best way to ensure that you are not one of the company owners who are left far behind and are left begging for rescue on the rocks.

Your Business is More Attractive Than You Think

Are you the owner of a business that aspires to grow but lacks the essential staff, partnerships, or ideas? You're approaching retirement age, yet you're making the typical mistake of assuming that no one would want to acquire your firm. You intend to pass it on to the next generation, but you are unaware that there are interested parties waiting in the wings to take over and breathe new life into the firm. Beginning with a notion and establishing a business around it is a more difficult task. Geoffroy A. Moore's great book Crossing the Chasm eloquently captures the insane cult of going up that cliff edge and needing to jump over the abyss to get to the other side. You'll need all your sheer willpower to get over the abyss. Be ready to captivate prospective investors! Identifying and acquiring the right investor for your situation is critical if you want to be successful in obtaining private equity. This book will help you achieve that aim. Before delving into the intricacies of your company's finances, it is critical that we first understand the workings of private equity and the variables that motivate investors to participate in certain firms but not others. You will discover why going the private equity route is in your company's best interests, as well as how this approach works in a real-world business setting. You'll also discover how to avoid the pirate equity types that hide in the shadowy corners of the financial industry, waiting to prey on founders and entrepreneurs who are ignorant of the ways in which private equity might hurt them. The second thing this book will do for you is introduce you to some individuals who work in the financial business and show you how to speak their specialized language in order to get their support. Also, it can aid you in selecting the right investment partner. Participating in this invitation-only club will provide you with knowledge about the private equity industry as well as the opportunity to network with the "money magicians," who have the ability to transform your company from a source of income into a source of financial security for future generations. Last but not least, you will learn the ins and outs of the written investment proposal as well as how to properly prepare for and present at the investor meeting. If you become "investment ready," you will discover what you need to put in place to attract the investors you want. The most crucial thing you will learn from Money Magnet is how your company can break open the private equity safe and bring in the money it deserves.

Chapter 2

THE BIG DIFFERENCE: OTHER PEOPLE'S MONEY

In the commercial world, momentum is important. Woody Allen, a film director, is credited with making the comparison between a relationship and a shark, noting that it must either evolve or die. Although Mr. Allen is not the most reputable expert on relationships, he does know how to communicate his arguments, which is very valuable in the business world. It is tough to convert from a business model that only supports the owner's lifestyle to one that thrives beyond the person, yet doing so might mean the difference between a company's survival and doom.

Private equity partners may be a great source of money, but they can also be a source of skill that can give your firm the extra impetus it needs to expand.

Other People's Money Gets You Moving

Are you confident that moving forward is what you want to do? Every company, even those that are struggling, has potential that may be realized with a capital influx from third parties. These opportunities might be capitalized on with the assistance of third-party investors (OPM). When you are starting to play golf for the first time in front of the best players in the club, the process of gaining investment may seem equally intimidating. You're undoubtedly familiar with the sensation of being stuck in a rut. Your organization may have been entangled in an eddy. You can no longer avoid the open waters by keeping concealed; the time has come to emerge from concealment and join the flow of water heading towards the raging ocean. It's time to start looking for possible investors. If you own a business, you are undoubtedly familiar with the concept of private equity financing. You are also presumably aware that this kind of financing is becoming an increasingly popular alternative for business owners in North America. You probably don't want to utilize OPM because of the bizarre and horrible story that the media loves to portray, in which the owners start off with high hopes but are subsequently proven to be bankrupt. Since it sells newspapers and magazines, the media likes to tell this narrative. "There are the common assumptions," says Markus Loft, an entrepreneur-in-residence at Rayna Capital recognized for his inexhaustible energy and excitement. The following are some popular urban legends. You, the business owner, have invested your entire life savings into your company, and you are now terrified that if you bring on partners, they will take control of the company, convince you to do things you would never do even if you were drunk, and trick you into signing away your life so that they can take it over and leave you homeless and destitute. Loft has said that "Once you have the check for the venture capital in your hands, there are stories of the unimaginable occurring. There are stories of private equity investors who went from a passionate love affair to a controlling marriage, sacrificing everything good in their life to get their greedy hands on your riches." While Loft admits, "Yes, there are some rattlesnakes in the sphere of business, as there are in other realms of life," she does so solemnly. There are opportunists and profiteers hiding in the shadows, ready to damage businesses to profit quickly from the transaction. These investors compel the business to employ a new management team that shares Vlad the Impaler's ethical values. They are careless about whether your bookkeeper, Stan, has been there for you through good and bad times. There is a shadowy section of the stock market inhabited by "pirates" who, rather than following their emotions, follow calculators that are directly tied to quarterly results. This market segment is known as "the dark side." Yet, in today's extremely competitive marketplaces, these private equity companies' track records will not last long. Loft contends that management that is just driven by financial gain is bound to failure because it lacks a sense of purpose. "There should be no doubt about that; the power is entirely in your hands. At this time, you are the organization's leader."

Time to Take Your Business Further

Every entrepreneur will ultimately reach a moment in their company's development when they have exhausted all their options. To begin, it is vital to understand that each organization has a life cycle. A company's development may be broken down into several phases of growth, ranging from a one-man band to a group with four guitars and a set of drums, all the way up to a full-fledged performance replete with a back-up orchestra and selling out Carnegie Hall. A one-man band, for example, may grow into a group with four guitars and a set of drums. Some enterprises never progress past the "one man with a guitar" stage. Second, if you are serious about obtaining growth finance from sources other than banks, you will need to change your mindset. You need to step outside of yourself. When the Beatles were at the peak of their success, they discovered that much of their music was being drowned out by their listeners' shrieks of pleasure. Therefore, they made the unexpected choice to stop touring and record the majority of their songs in a studio. That makes no logic and is just insane! There aren't many other artists who would pass up such a simple way to improve their earnings. The Fab Four also arrived at another key decision. They surrounded themselves with professional managers who had similar creative aspirations and complementing abilities to have individuals who would support and, in fact, accelerate their success. Because of their dedication to their creative history, the Beatles were able to transcend their beginnings as a rock-and-roll touring group; therefore, their music will survive all of us. They would not have achieved the same degree of fame or wealth if they had retained all decision-making power inside their original band and had not sought support from other sources. There is no room for mistake here: fund managers and venture capitalists seek firms that seem to be successful investments. They want to invest in a firm where you have strong personal dedication and enthusiasm. They are searching for leaders who are passionate about building a legacy that will last long after they are gone. Do you want to let your firm grow beyond your control at this stage in your career? You are the sort of person who is ambitious enough to want your firm to survive even after you are gone. You're aware of how rapidly time goes. With the aid of private equity, your firm may be transformed from an asset that just supports a lifestyle to a professional enterprise that can afford the degree of rigor required to make it up to the public stock market. If you have private equity specialists on your board, such as Markus Loft, you may benefit from his expertise and experience as the business grows, since he has been there and can share it with you. If your firm obtains private equity backing, its prospects of success increase dramatically.

What Will Make or Break You

The shocking truth is that your attitude toward possible outside investors may be the single most important element in predicting whether you will be successful in securing finance. "80 percent of proposals are turned down mainly due to the mindset of the guy presenting the presentation," says serial entrepreneur Alan McMillan. "Private equity investors do not want to work with someone who is not a team player because entrepreneurs are stubborn, do not listen, and do not want to work with someone who is not a team player." Do you believe an investor will behave authoritatively? Someone like Donald Trump telling you what to do You're worried that I'm not bringing in enough money to keep investors happy. It's likely that you don't comprehend the financial markets and have never investigated prospects outside of the bank. These are all very common worries, and your ego is causing you to feel this way. To be ready for investors, you must first understand what it takes to put your ego aside and share control to progress up the development curve and become a Stage 3 Legacy Enterprise. Then and only then will you be ready to receive investment funds. A graphical representation of the development that needs to occur for you, the leader, to progress from the stage of a sapling to that of a fully grown upright evergreen tree.

Stage 1: Product

Regardless of whether the owner is an engineer, scientist, or baker, the owner's specialized expertise is the most important aspect of the company's success in the first stage, product. The engineer, scientist, or pie-making expert is trained to think and speak in the language of their favorite product, whether it's technology, science, or loaves of bread. The eyes do what they do best: they discover new technology, create new drugs, and make award-winning French bread. Many smart individuals remain at this level because they are enthralled with their product and, to be honest, are rather adept at being experts. The eyes feel that the product is so powerful that it will sell itself. These individuals do not get engrossed in managing their businesses or, all too often, themselves. If they're lucky, they'll find managers to handle all aspects of business development, such as administration, bookkeeping, marketing, and keeping an eye on the bottom line. Answer the following questions to determine your readiness to go on to the next level of business: 1. What is your definition of success? Are you in business to make money? Many people legitimately want a 9-to-5 to job so they can play in the jazz band on Mondays, attend their child's soccer game,

volunteer, or whatever. There is no place at the top if you are in business for the sake of your lifestyle.
2. Are you doing this for the sake of your ego? Most entrepreneurs begin with the intention of making money and running their business. According to research, if you do not select which is more essential, you will end up neither rich nor in charge of a powerful firm. When the time comes, be able to bring in partners and share ownership to go to the next level.
3. Do you think you could perform a better job for someone else? Engineers may develop the finest technology, but it will never be purchased by a customer because it is just too dangerous to award the job to a tiny, unproven firm. Because of the sheer power of its brand, Thumb would do more if it operated under the umbrella of a bigger organization that could patent its ideas and bring them to market quicker.
4. How are you doing with your cash flow, Flow? Do you make assumptions regarding money coming in and going out in your company strategy (if you have one)? Consider the suggestion to "double the contractor's estimate of time and expense" when planning a home remodel. This also applies to business planning.
5. Is money important? That certainly does. You must charge for your services to pay your bills. Otherwise, you are a hobbyist rather than an entrepreneur. The most difficult skill is convincing someone to put her hand in her pocket and pay you money. Great entrepreneurs get customers to pay for more and more.

Stage 2: Owner-Controlled

A more formal structure is required for a Stage 2 owner-controlled company. Knowledge is accumulated around a product or service and formalized into formal strategies, rules, plans, and budgets to enable more people to produce the product. Stage 2 includes marketing strategy, financial systems, and operational methodologies, among other things. You may show that your management team's abilities extend beyond the "product coolness" emphasis of Stage 1. The "doing more" forces your company to evolve from a single man with a hamburger stand to a branded McDonald's chain, or from a single bakery to Ace Bakery supplying French loaves to grocery chains, or from a club of programmers sharing photographs for fun to Flickr (a Canadian start-up eventually bought out by Yahoo! Inc. in 2005).Even with processes and controls in place, a Stage 2 owner-controlled firm may not be ready for formal investors. Here's the problem with attracting financing: the distinction the difference in performance between Stage 2 and Stage 3 businesses is the leader's thinking. It all begins with you. Stage 3 Legacy leaders are ambitious enough to set aside their egos to build a company that can thrive without them always sitting in the captain's chair. The eyes see that for the firm to develop, they must go beyond being the lone star and embrace the change brought about by private equity investors.

Stage 3: Legacy

The Stage 3 Legacy Company refers to a company that is best positioned to attract private equity, particularly venture capital. Leaders of Stage 3 legacy firms understand their company's progress. The eyes acknowledge that changes will be necessary to progress to legacy status, one of which is an equity partnership. The owner-entrepreneur who makes the deliberate choice to migrate from an owner-controlled to a legacy firm will realize that private equity partners may help them reach the next level of wealth.

New Rules for Your Leadership Style

Participants on American Idol, whether they like it or not, must endure pitiless and public evaluations of their performances from a panel of judges. The judge's duty is not to instruct the performers but to determine which singers can sell many recordings and hence earn money. Ultimately, judge Simon Cowell has invested his own money in good performances. Yet, most singers (and most of the audience) look perplexed by Simon's position, requesting slobbering approval as if he were their patient, supportive instructor. Wrong. An article recounts the numerous cringeworthy singers who fiercely replied to Simon's critique by saying, "What do you know, anyway?" (A lot about what it takes to persuade music fans to pay twenty bucks for an album.) These sulky singers would have benefited considerably more by listening and aggressively prodding Simon for further remarks, since he is clearly worth hearing out—albeit mercilessly and bluntly. Take a long, deep breath and gaze into the mirror. Do you consider feedback to be a major assault? Do you fire a rocket at your enemies, thinking, "That'll show them?" A private equity collaboration starts with Simon's enthusiasm and candor. Investors will hold you up to the harsh, ruthless light of day to see whether your company has the potential to produce money in the future. They will not guide you on your next actions or how to improve while they are deciding whether to give you, their money. Will you be able to listen when their remarks begin to flow? Will you advance to the next round, or will you be one of the Idol wannabes frantically stomping off the stage, too insecure—hear the reality criticisms you so desperately need? "Ninety-five percent of people are not born to be entrepreneurs," argues serial entrepreneur Alan McMillan. "The eye would get too disheartened by all the rejection to continue. Those that succeed, on the other hand, can receive criticism well, dismissing it as water off a duck's back while simultaneously absorbing the important ideas. Entrepreneurs that are emotionally developed may get financing. Emotional regulation is something that can be learned.

Can You Attract First-Round Money?

Unsurprisingly, the start-up business devotes a significant amount of effort to Stage 1, Product. Yet, to attract the next round of funding (from venture capitalists or private equity fund managers), the owner must go at least to Stage 2. To go from the initial rest level of the product onward, you must overcome a fundamental quandary. Explain honestly and as soon as possible how you define success. Is it more important to be the king of the joint or to make money? According to Noam Wasserman's research, save for a few celebrities like Richard Branson and Anita Roddick, it is uncommon for entrepreneurs to carry their firm to a durable and affluent level of business. "An entrepreneur who gives up more stock to persuade investors develops a more valued organization than one who departs with less," says Wasserman. If you decide to make money, you will realize that there will come a time when you will be unable to do it alone and will need to pass over stock to partners.

The second round of financing is often focused on the business plan, a two-minute description of the company's purpose (the elevator pitch), and a PowerPoint presentation. The entrepreneur who can combine business competence with emotional maturity that appeals to investors—Level 3, which is Legacy—is the one who is most likely to acquire approval, regardless of the amount of development. The aforementioned CEOs handle all of the stages in Stages 1 and 2, but acknowledge that the important choice to invest will be made only if they can accept rejection of their ideas and businesses, learn from remarks, and understand that recruiting investors is a luxury.

When you participate in the negotiating process, you will be tested to see whether you can learn (are you inquisitive about other new methods of doing business rather than grimacing uncomfortably at suggestions, as if your mother had just asked if you'd washed your teeth and cleaned your room?). The investor is monitoring your response to curve balls and interrogative remarks from the first

point of contact. Do you get defensive? Are you sensitive to questions about prior performance, making excuses for what occurred rather than thoroughly exploring the matter? Do you accept opposing viewpoints? Are you an attentive listener? The answers to these personal questions will help investors decide if they want to engage with you over the next few years. Despite the criticism, reality television has a devoted following because viewers are drawn in by the direct human touch. If American Idol isn't your thing, check out CBC's Dragons' Den, where seasoned, self-made billionaires listen to early-stage, firm entrepreneurs pitch for investment funds. Kevin O'Leary, the scariest dragon, feels that the boss's demeanor while being questioned by investors is the most important factor in attracting investment. "I don't know why fate smiles on some and lets the others go," he says, "but maybe the answer lies in the strength that person learns in coping with rejection."

The New Competitive Advantage: Skills

Stage 3 legacy corporations understand that with the availability of private equity to smaller firms, a CEO's number one talent must shift from obtaining cash to assembling the world's top talents. Capital has been turned into a commodity over the last two decades. Savvy company owners and CEOs understand that their ability to work with outstanding people will provide them with a competitive edge in the future. The beauty of private equity is that it shares financial risk while also providing an exceptional range of creative contributors to collaborate and risk fresh ideas (some wacky, some odd) to create the business. How do you determine whether to pursue private equity? The question itself is insufficient. That must be related to a second question: How do you measure success? "I want to merge with private equity and get a lot of money," you say, rubbing your hands together and grinning like Jim Carrey. Or are you the Stage 3 CEO who vows, "I want to establish a lasting legacy—a firm that runs without me?"

Face Up to Your Financial Reality

You may profit from extra money and competent stewardship whether you are part of a family-run firm, a lone entrepreneur, or a manager in a neglected corporate division. Diversifying your assets may be a good idea if you want to develop your firm, minimize your risk exposure, or both. Private equity allows you to take some money off the table so that your firm does not account for all your net worth. Some owners do it early in the firm, while others do it at the end. "CEOs who join up with private equity firms sometimes wind up having 99% of their net worth in their company—the equivalent of putting all your money into one stock," says Canterbury Park Management's Greg Milevsky. "A CEO who joins a fund now has the option of pulling some money out to diversify elsewhere while still benefiting from the discipline that private equity offers to the development of their firm." Owning your own company is extremely personal, and you are not alone in being hesitant to bring in partners since it will force you to confront your financial reality. It is a scorecard that displays your degree of achievement, and most owners, whether they are making six figures or not, believe that their scorecard should be bigger, better, and more remarkable. You go to the doctor when you need professional guidance on a specific health condition. You may be ashamed to bring up your "issue" before the test. Yet, after the doctor has a description of your symptoms, you generally feel relieved and a lot more at peace knowing what is really going on. You may even question why you believed you couldn't deal with the "issue." Private equity follows a similar pattern. Are you terrified of being told no, your company isn't worth that much, you're a washed-up, you'll never retire, and you've squandered your life? If you are a sales-focused entrepreneur who overlooks the company's future in noncoal development, you will make expensive blunders. Do not make the typical error of believing that your firm lacks the potential to attract investors just because you cannot see it. Trust me, if you must pay clients, there will be interest.

Make the Two Most Important Decisions

"Fine," says the Stage 3 Legacy owner, "I want to see this company grow rapidly. This is not an owner-managed company. " I want to see how far this firm can go—even to the Fortune 500." To pursue the Stage 3 legacy and seek private equity partners is a basic and very personal choice since each owner has a vastly different set of decision criteria and risk constraints. It is difficult to achieve Level 3 and take on private equity without answering two questions honestly: Choice 1: Do I need to have personal control over the business? Do I feel personally secure in a collaboration with strong, skilled individuals? Will I be able to let go of control? Do I have what it takes to be a team player? Is success defined by managing my own team, or can I step back to share power or even leave the CEO role? Choice 2: What amount of risk am I willing to take? How much of this firm do I want to own? Could I do more for the company with other people's money (OPM)? How much money does the company really need—$500,000, $1M, $2M, $5M, $10M, $21M, or more? How much do I want my partners to assist me? Would you want me to lower my risk by selling 25% or 75% of my company's stock?

Decision 1: If Personal Control Comes First

A food firm in the United States of America desired to expand and establish a new factory ten years ago. When the CEO phoned Ed Riechelmann, who now heads up True North Investments, for a meeting, it was close to signing up private equity partners, with 51% ownership going to private equity partners. "You know, folks, I've been running this company by myself for twenty years, and I don't believe I'm capable of answering to anybody else," he stated. I don't believe I'd be a good partner. I was delighted at first, but then I realized I'm too set in my ways. I'm going to continue with bank debt, which needs no effort on my part." This tenacious entrepreneur understood he was a Stage 2 firm and was willing to remain the captain of his own ship. A Stage 3 owner would be ambitious enough to set aside his ego and step aside to let other professionals provide strategic advice. This food firm specialist realized he had gone as far as he could on his own. He realized that for his company to go to the next level of financing, he would need partners, but he chose to stick with what he knew and could manage. He was afraid that if he opened the door to private equity, the horse might run, with equity as the unexpected jockey holding the whip and rushing out into the distance. "We value that owner's candor," Riechelmann adds. "Absolutely. When working with private equity, it is critical to grasp what it means to be a partner." Private equity, according to Riechelmann, is not for owners who value personal control above everything else.

The Dilemma of Leadership

The irony of owner-run businesses is that their present success is often due to their dictatorial leadership style. The difficulty of progressing to Stage 3 is adjusting to a team of peer's partners and learning together. It will not be an easy progression, and there will be wounded egos yours included. The same dominant ego and personality that pushed, prodded, and tugged the firm to its present level will need to be reined in and even set aside by its founders. Only then will they be ready to invite partners. Well, it's ironic, and it's exceedingly difficult to pull off. Stage 3 business leaders recognize the paradox of future success: shifting from autocracy to cooperation will help the firm develop. Nevertheless, it may be painfully difficult for company owners to accept partners. Stage 3 entails focusing on integrative abilities that will serve as the basis for a legacy company. Integrative abilities like cooperation, listening, and the capacity to grow by absorbing criticism without feeling threatened are required to integrate a skilled team into a unified vision that creates a legacy. The owner of the food business enjoyed his owner-controlled lifestyle and would not be able to bear other people telling him what to do—or so he thought. He did not wish to expand the company beyond its existing size. He was content where he was. But he may be leaving a lot of money on the table as well as passing up a chance to develop the company and maybe grow as a person.

Decision 2: Your Level of Investment and Risk

The second question that company owners or CEOs must ask themselves is how much personal risk they are prepared to accept. Since they make all of the choices and control the majority of the firm, the risk profile of the food company's corporation is elevated. What would happen if he was run over by a bus? His firm would not have perished if he had strategic partners in the private equity sector. It's conceivable that his family and coworkers feel glad that the threat has spread. There is also the tension that comes with growing a business. The chief executive officer of a manufacturing business was entirely absorbed in his job and happy with his

company's success. Nevertheless, after hearing a speech delivered by Apple's creator, Steve Jobs, his drive to develop the firm grew. The CEO was aware that he had the essential ambition, but he was hesitant to risk so much of his own money. He had the financial resources to take the risk, but he couldn't access the public markets at the time. The company's CEO chose to aid the company's development by selling 75% of the company's shares to private equity partners. They helped to grow the staff, build the processes, and find possible acquisitions. He ended up obtaining a better financial return on his 25% stake in the firm than he would have earned if he had retained the full company for himself. How tremendously satisfying it must be when the most difficult way also turns out to be the most successful! If you are going to follow Steve Jobs' advice, you must be mindful of the possible downsides connected with expanding. Another thing to think about: Steve Jobs was fired from Apple for a decade, but he argues that the firm was able to thrive because of the private equity financial partners who were already in place.
The amount of hazard varies. A medical equipment maker planned to launch a brand-new product. The owner, who knew it would cost $5 million to bring it to market, weighed the risks involved. "Right now, I'm seated at the pro table. If everything goes as planned, the product will increase the value of my company from $10 million to $30 million, with a one-million-dollar cash flow. If things don't go as planned, I'll be out $5,000,000, and it'll take me five years to make up for it and get back to where I started. Pass! On the other hand, private equity partners will be pulled in by the promise of growth. They get a sight of the enormous fish in the murky water and enjoy the sparkle of its scales; they will pick up the harpoon and go through the fight, bleeding from gripping the line and facing incredible difficulties to bring home the fish that others can only admire from the beach. The CEO of a medical device company chose to be open about the conservative nature of both his personal and financial goals. "I began this business in my garage, and it now has to be able to run without me. Let's start a company together and share the risk." He was able to walk away with enough money to pay for his retirement and compensate for all of the lean years, but he was still able to stay around to experience the new growth with the partners who contributed vital

new abilities such as vision, connections, and patient capital through the storm. He was able to get enough money off the table to pay for his retirement and make up for all of the hard times.

Decrease Ownership but Gain Growth

When you are the owner of a company, your level of risk is determined by the number of shares you sell to a private equity firm. It is essential to recognize that the level of effort that the fund will apply to your income growth is entirely at your control. You have the option of selling either 100% or 90% of the business and walking away from it. If you sell 90% of the company, you can maintain part of the shares while also getting some of the upside from the new ownership. Seventy-five percent, so you can maintain some control while also benefiting from the expertise and heroic effort that your new partners are putting in. Thirty percent and take on a minority shareholder; for that price, you cannot expect these partners to be actively involved in the business in any significant way. There is no way that private equity partners will be encouraged to put in a lot of work when they will only receive 30 percent of the returns. Stage 3 owners understand that the greater the investor's stake in the company, the greater the effort the investor will put forth to assist in the growth of sales. It is not up to the private equity fund but up to you to make this choice. You oversee the situation. The degree of ownership that your financial partners have will have a direct bearing on the amount of drive and expertise you may anticipate from them.

Chapter 3

TAKING ON A PRIVATE EQUITY PARTNER: HOW IT WORKS

A Case Study: Sassy Seeds

When a company called Sassy Seeds saw a drop in earnings for the first time in its existence, the owner, Tom, blamed it on the rise of the Canadian dollar. The sharp decrease that happened in the second year demonstrated Tom's incapacity to continue dismissing the thought that danger was on the horizon. Tom's leadership of Sassy Seeds has been nothing short of ferocious up until this point. He was following in his grandfather's footsteps, who had created the company with the slogan "Keep up with the future since business is always unexpected." He was doing so because he was following in his grandfather's footsteps. Didn't Tom do that before? Tom was the first in his business to automate seed packing and boldly go where no seed grower had gone before using information technology. As a consequence, Tom was always at the top of his field. As soon as the lucrative potential of the internet became accessible, Tom posted the Sassy Seeds catalog. This enabled him to instantly penetrate new foreign markets. When a British online gardening club picked Daisy Glory from Sassy Seeds as the winner of their "best seed" award for the first time, you'd think Tom's team had won the Stanley Cup. Despite all of this good intent and a wonderful workforce operating production processes and marketing strategies, earnings were plummeting at an alarming pace. One evening, Tom was attending a meeting of his CEO Group Advisory when he learned about "paradigm shifts." That was a difficult confession for him to make, but he admitted that his clientele no longer had the time or room to cultivate. China was also eating away at his earnings, but he had no idea what to do. As a consequence of all of these considerations, he felt a greater sense of urgency to sell the firm before sales fell like

wild lemmings plunging down a cliff. He sighed, "This is so over," and picked up the phone to contact a private equity firm that had spoken at a conference he had attended. "It's over," he thought. When the investor, Mr. Private Equity, came up to Tom's packaging business ready to become a partner and assured Tom that there was no need to sell the whole thing, no one could have been more surprised. Tom was the only one who was taken aback. Tom had no notion at the time that, despite selling 75% of his stock in the business, the remaining 25% of his ownership would one day be worth more than the company's entire value prior to the sale. Tom was glad to take a large sum of money off the table to fund his retirement, but he was concerned about giving up equity while remaining CEO. He was curious how things would go with Mr. Private Equity as his new partner. Would it be a collaboration like Scully and Mulder from the X-Files, taking on hidden rival forces together? Or would it be more of a master-servant relationship, with the investor acting as the Lone Ranger and Tom as Tonto? Or would he end up becoming a firebrand? What strategy would Mr. Private Equity recommend? It would be dishonest to claim that it was easy; Tom battled greatly during his first year on the job. Initially, there were production issues, such as changes in housekeeping, that Tom chastised himself for not addressing sooner. Yet it was Mr. Private Equity's use of language, not his meticulous notetaking and desire for minutiae, that persuaded Tom that he was lying. "We need to concentrate on a few key indicators that are easily understood by everyone and are posted on our operating dashboard." After a while, Tom unwillingly started keeping track of statistics, and he reluctantly admitted that this information helped his crew when Sassy Seeds got off track. Tom also reluctantly recognized that this information was useful. As Tom saw that his team required him less and was able to describe the activities that created income and expenses independently, he concluded that what was measured was what was completed. Since their techniques were disjointed, bored salesmen had to be replaced when the stats were eventually correct. Priorities are now defined by customer support representatives and individual account managers. They do this by estimating the number of calls that must be answered and selecting the most valuable customers. Stars who had previously been neglected were rewarded with sales-targeted remuneration, which gave them an additional boost and encouraged them even more. The quantity of money earned progressively increased. After ten months, Tom had to admit that the monthly board meetings with Mr. Private Equity and the two fund managers were wearing on his nerves due to their emphasis on bringing a degree of discipline to the firm that it had never known before. It did grate on his nerves when members of his management team expressed their appreciation for the changes. The only focus at this stage was increasing the quantity of money earned. Tom was conscious that he had failed to see the forest for the trees, and he was disappointed that it had taken his new business partners so long to understand that the rise in manufacturing costs indicated that they should include China in their packaging technique. Mr. Private Equity's new systems (which he had fought) were also responsible for exposing the expenditure difficulties.

Some investors want to help you grow your business at a pace faster than 20% per year, while others want 25% or even more.

Before you send out a frightened scream, consider that private equity investors may help you achieve this growth rate. Even though not all investors have previous experience in the industry in which your business works, those who do will, if they are interested in your company, use methods and techniques that have worked for them in the past and will bring that success to your organization as well. They may provide you with an experienced CFO and point you in the direction of new business prospects. Along the way, they will urge you to overcome your fear of success (or failure, or whatever), to overcome the hurdles that have been impeding your development, and to finish the necessary duties. With the assistance of Mr. Private Equity and the capacity to develop forward-looking financial models offered by his newly recruited CFO, the team undertook an examination of the firm for the first time, looking at what brought in the cash and where it was spent. They collaborated to develop a high-level strategy for moving forward. Tom had never imagined it was even somewhat possible. Mr. Private Equity used to write out the company's annual goals in his office and then debate them with his senior leadership team while playing golf before implementing his new way of governance. He argued that it was not important for everyone to be informed of the company's future (he was afraid it would scare them). David, the operations manager, was now excitedly making recommendations for ways for the firm to grow. Mr. Private Equity's blue-chip executive search firm found the new Chief Operating Officer (COO), who used his exceptional expertise operating organizations in a range of foreign locales. Mr. Private Equity advised Tom that "private equity is particularly adept at accessing a huge network of specialists and businesspersons, who can be made available to assist Sassy Seeds." Tom was taken aback by this. The addition of fresh personnel boosted Sassy Seeds' morale and resulted in a 180-degree turnaround in their strategic approach. Rather than producing seeds, they now get specimens from Mr. Private Equity's worldwide network, in this instance vendors in both China and South America, and package them under the Sassy brand. This technique has given the team more time to concentrate on boosting sales and diversifying the packaging designs offered. Tom was aware that Sassy Seeds' five-year development goal should have been written out years ago, but, for some reason, this never occurred. Each manager at Sassy Seeds has distinct objectives to help the firm come closer to its aim. Please keep in mind that Mr. Private Equity is not a celestial being. The approach itself encouraged Tom and his team to focus on the tasks that would have the largest impact on the project. The incident then occurred. Mr. Private Equity noted at the start of a board of directors meeting that "Sassy Seeds has a big difficulty with its conventional line of business." Mr. Private Equity had not yet been finished when Tom gained an unexpected interest. "We have a proposition for the whole team. "Are you up for it?" Tom thought it was time to address an issue that had been bugging him for quite some time. "Aren't we whistling as we pass by the cemetery? Isn't the industry in which Sassy Seeds operates on the decline?" Mr. Private Equity's eyes were drawn to Tom. "I like how open you are. Nonetheless, Sassy Seeds is a great brand name that can be used for a range of products. But what about the flow of money? How are we going to be able to fund further projects? Tom, you seem to have forgotten we're not a bank, replied Mr. Private Equity, laughing, and leaning back in his chair. We base our choice to provide finance on anticipated prospects rather than existing income. A typical firm was obliged to change its product offering, but the brand name was strong enough to sustain the addition of new things. This is only an unforeseen hiccup in the road, my buddy, and I've been through much worse. We have a game plan for the next five years that gives us the freedom to abandon the usual method and pursue an altogether other path. After hearing the word "patient capital" for the first time, Tom finally understood what it meant. The sensation of relief that washed over him was so great that he felt as if he had just hit a home run. He was frustrated by the amount of time and effort necessary to create a thorough five-year plan in which future revenues were specified down to the precise amount that should be spent on marketing brochures. Understandably, he was aware that the private equity firm assigned a value to his business and gave him shares based on what they expected the company to generate in the future rather than what it had earned before. The financial future's goal had been set, but market circumstances were moving faster than planned. There were still four years to complete the plan, and Tom was beginning to realize that his ideas were not the only way forward. Rather, there were alternatives. With serious purpose, he inspected the five-year targets and listened as Mr. Private Equity read aloud the top line, which was the purchase of an industry supplier. "Never in a million years did I imagine I'd be buying a company," Tom said. Tom and Sarah, the CEO of Lots of Pots, a garden container company identified by the private equity fund team as a prospective acquisition target, were supposed to meet for lunch. Tom's first response was suspicion (to put it mildly). Yet he was shocked to see that they got along like two peas in a pod. At lunch, Mr. Private Equity outlined his concept, which was for Sassy Seeds to provide Lots of Pots with seeds to plant in their pots. Since the Sassy Seeds brand was more well-known, the tags on the arrangements would say "Sassy Seed—Garden in a Container." Several Pots helped to the party's success by providing outstanding marketing ties with new clients, particularly all the key stores. They were also masters in the logistics of transporting little pallets of merchandise to a variety of locations around the nation. Tom would never have delegated another expert; thus Mr. Private Equity's lawyer saw the arrangement through to completion and signing. Over the summer, Tom and Sarah were surprised by how quickly their rapid flowerpots for patios, front doors, and apartment balconies were picked up by clients. At the golf club, Tom's pals made fun of him for the multiple positive media articles that included photographs of a joyful Tom cradling a Sassy Seeds balcony pot of flowers and gushing descriptions of his company's dramatic transformation, all of which were orchestrated by Mr. Private Equity. Sassy, however, was now selling seeds at around 10 times the prior price since she had successfully combined them in a variety of pots. When Mr. Private Equity was brought on board to offer centralised purchasing and technical knowledge, the margins grew dramatically. Tom agreed to Mr. Private Equity's idea that Sarah take over as CEO as part of the new Succession Plan to buy out Tom's remaining 25% ownership when he retires in three years as a reward for her difficult work. This was part of the revised Succession Plan, which included buying out Tom's remaining 25% stake. Sarah had proven herself. Tom couldn't keep his enthusiasm in check. Tom told his wife over chardonnay on the terrace that it "got my goat" that someone else could develop his business and manage the people who worked there. However, for the time being, Mr. Private Equity has my support and vote. Tom was aware that the private equity team's advice was considerably different from the character from Wall Street's mechanical and "ignore all people" economic approach, often known as the Gordon Gecko caricature, which is so famous in Hollywood. Tom was convinced that Sassy Seeds would not only survive but also thrive because of Mr. Private Equity's engagement.

The video Sassy Seeds is a collection of genuine tales from various firms, and it serves as an example of the method used by KKR and Bain, which has raised the bar in terms of how to invest funds. This is the ideal situation, which other private investors are pursuing, with varied degrees of success. Figure 3.1 explains how private equity might offer value to your firm in the same way as the example of Sassy Seeds and the other instances that will follow indicate how private equity could provide value to your company. Please keep in mind that your purchase will not contain all the value-added features shown in the table. It is conceivable that you will just get a few. Realize that this is the greatest level imaginable. In choosing your business partners, have a copy of "The Private Equity Value-Add" list on hand and be sure to ask prospective investors what they can do to aid your firm.

Are You Ready for Private Equity?

If you are starting a long-standing family company or currently manage one, the first thing you need to do is establish a rigorous and demanding advisory board. Hold a discussion with them about the demands and desires of investors. It might be tough to prepare for the search for an investor since each investor is a member of a fund with its own unique set of talents, dynamics, ideology, and amount of work to undertake. The action will take multiple abrupt twists.

If you can explain why, you and your team are the ideal people for the job, how your company is doing well with a clear path ahead, and how your technology has a strong niche yet there are barriers to entry, you are ready. Are you able to express the sector's difficulties while still underscoring its potential and benefits? To determine a fair price for the transaction, you must have an accurate grasp of the worth of your firm. To reaffirm what has already been mentioned, the most crucial thing is that you and your team perform well. Investors invest their money in people rather than technology or things because they understand that people create value. Nevertheless, as Adam Smith emphasizes in his book "The Wealth of Nations," it is the emotions of human beings that drive business and its consequences. We will create your presentation to investors towards the conclusion of the book, which is where most finance textbooks begin. But, since your emotions will have a direct influence on the success of your investments, it is more necessary to spend your time learning about investor viewpoints than it is to write a thorough business strategy. Even before you start your presentation, the investor will have decided if they like you enough to consider giving you money. Empathy for the needs of others is an important aspect of bringing people around to your side. Collaboration of money and skills Company owners must know themselves personally their talents, weaknesses, and goals but many do not go beyond the box and analyse their financial risk. Are they storing their wealth in a non-liquid form (i.e., the company) in order to maintain their lifestyle? Are they putting off the transfer of their company to a professional one? Are they passing up a chance to expand the brand on a global scale? Most importantly, will distributing the risk among partners assist their families?

Challenging You

As you decide whether to extend your firm, you may feel uneasy, offended by the prospect of the intrusion of investors. Is it conceivable that you are perceiving that you are out of your league and fear the challenge? If so, the evidence reveals you are not alone. Private equity investors may be younger than you or their career route may have given them a great lot more exposure to the large corporate world than you. The eye also has made more money. They have operated their own firm and sold it, and now wish to invest their money; some are skilled money managers with strategic knowledge. This can all be daunting things for entrepreneurs' content in their industry.

Here is what you need to understand. These equity investors often have the foresight to ask you all those sacred-cow questions that your staff may not have the confidence to ask. This forthrightness will certainly annoy some owners. However, if you dig down deep you will realize that anger is the cover for a deeper emotion fear of being discovered to be out of your depth. Testing your company against those of an investor may sound intimidating because it implies you will be judged possibly chastised. It suggests things will certainly change and the business may no longer be within your control.

The Company You Keep

When asked how to build a successful firm by a young student, financial genius Warren Buffett famously said, "How do you make a fantastic business?" Buffs Tet's counsel was to "surround oneself with good people." If you strive to obtain exposure to the males who work in private equity, you may profit from Buff Tet's expertise. You'll notice that individuals around you have a new, infectious level of ambition. As Warren Buffett would say, there is nothing wrong with acknowledging that you are intimidated. It is advantageous to be urged to investigate your organisation in ways that you have previously avoided. These seasoned investors possess the required skills to help you in bringing your business to the next level. These will be the motivation that drives you to utilise your "Spidey senses" in ways you were previously unaware were even possible, transforming you from a successful businessperson into a superhero. Sharing resources such as expertise, contact networks, processes, and supply chains, as well as setting milestones, expanding markets beyond familiar geographical borders, and developing innovative methods of producing goods, all contribute to the creation of additional value within private equity partnerships. Owners typically struggle to look beyond their own horizon or ambitions because they wrongly feel that their own degree of competence and network is the highest that can be reached appropriately. This is very understandable. They may be unaware that, at their heart, private equity companies love the entrepreneurial spirit; these businesses want to partner with you rather than enforce power over you. Legacy company owners have reached the point where they understand what a cooperation with a private equity partner may look like. They see that this unique combination of resources, expertise, and talents will give an incredible competitive advantage that will far outweigh mere bank debt on a global scale. This is something they are aware of. They understand that "hanging out" with other eager and passionate private equity investors will encourage them to become even more enthused. What are your thoughts? Do you surround yourself with people that do not threaten you or attempt to encourage you, and then wonder why you can't go beyond where you are now? Do you believe it is feasible for you to work with individuals that make you nervous?

The Right Partner Adds Vision

When it comes to private equity, the role of the outsider with a clearer perception of the situation is critical. Have you ever observed that the filmmakers of the most authentic renderings of a country's culture are typically those who are not native to that country? Sam Mendes, a British producer, was in charge of the highly praised film American Beauty. Ismail Merchant, an indigenous British novelist, is the author of the famous historical playroom with a View. Similarly, an investment partner who recognizes the market power of a company's brand name and forms a new relationship is akin to this situation. There is a lot of misinformation about private equity investors since they are commonly mistaken for regular banking organizations. Bankers like to boast about their ties with their clients, but it's more like a parent talking to a teenager who is trying not to divulge any information at all. In contrast to typical bank funding, private equity does not entail either an employer-employee dynamic or a master-servant relationship between investors and enterprises. It is a partnership whose major goal is to increase the company's market value. Both are ready to take the risk of focusing their business energies on each other for the next five years. In contrast to banks, which may retrieve assets (such as buildings and equipment) and get a steady stream of monthly payments within a few months, the two might win big or lose everything.

What Investors Want

Partners in private equity want to know that you have done your research to understand why their method of financing is going to be beneficial to your business's expansion; in other words, why their methods are unique. They want you to appreciate them and be able to explain why they have a higher standing than other people who bring you money. The eyes want you to treat them as though they are special. The value of your company needs to significantly increase within the next four, five, or ten years for private equity investors to be interested. The only reason the value of your firm will skyrocket is that investors will bring in more skilled workers and more vitality to the business. According to Pete Peterson, Chairman of The Blackstone Group, "If you look at the typical private equity investment we make... the vast majority of the time we invest much more in the future, in development, and in research; because what we're interested in doing is doing those things that are going to make the companies go faster so that they'll be worth more than what we paid for them in five years." This shake-up will present a challenge for you, but if you have a solid understanding of the following important challenges for private equity investors, the road ahead will be easier to navigate.

A Motivated Board

The potential investor will be looking for a board that has good reporting capabilities, which are lacking in your company now. Your workplace will see the process because of this. You have the freedom to decide as an entrepreneur how much information to share. The board is not the team captain; rather, it is the squad's coach. Once you come to grips with the fact that board members are not in competition to be smarter than you and with the demand that they provide regular reports, you will understand that you are still the glue that makes the board a team. According to Bob Roy, the gentle bear leader of Rayna Capital, "some companies worry about having a fund manager take a seat on their board and interfere in the business." "Some companies worry about having a fund manager take a seat on their board and interfere in the business." "What CEOs may not appreciate is that the vast majority of funds do not intend to get their hands dirty and will instead focus their assistance on a strategic level," Bob continues by saying, "Owners rapidly come to recognize how the mere presence of the private equity partners on their board brings improved reputation and legitimacy to a corporation."

A component of the plan is to expand while simultaneously gaining access to money. If an analyst were to look at your finances, she would be looking for evidence of debt. The company runs the danger of remaining unmoved over time if its balance sheet is not "geared" (laden up) with debt. The golden rule regarding cash is that you must spend it or risk losing it. You need to have a healthy appetite for debt if you wish to expand into purchasing additional businesses. It demonstrates a lack of initiative in business to say to a potential investor, "I'm ungeared I have little debt." As the business grows, there will inevitably be a point when it is necessary to implement the discipline of loan repayments. This has the magical effect of forcing the management of large private equity partnerships to concentrate on cash flow. The team will concentrate like never before on quarterly payments, which are what gets a company doing the things it needs to do to bring in paying customers. The focus will be greater than it has ever been.

Recognition of Their Skills

A considerable number of private equity investors have been business owners, having taken their companies from Stage 2 Legacy to Stage 3 Legacy before selling them. Their financial investment in your company as well as the partnership that you have formed with them allows your firm to benefit from the invaluable lessons that are associated with expanding a business. Investors that are savvy have a lot of experience looking at a range of firms, talking to people who work in those organizations, analyzing their management practices and operational strategies, and talking to other people who work in those businesses. By incorporating their point of view into your firm, you will be able to acquire a more holistic understanding of aspects of your company that you may have overlooked. Because of this, they can add strategy, recruit personnel, and find strategic relationships.

The excited Greg Milevsky of Canterbury Park Management had this to say about private equity: "Once you pass the signing of the agreement, private equity influences everything in a business." The connection will always involve aspects such as marketing, operations, sales, and the management of the workforce. Private equity investors who are at the top of their game, like Jerry Schwartz, who is the CEO of Onex, are often referred to as the Renaissance people of business. This is because the most successful funds bring a tremendous degree of skill and industry knowledge to the table. To be successful, funds need to be equipped with a lot more than simple financial knowledge.

Recognition That Their Risk Is as Big as Yours

The people that invest in private equity want you to be aware that they are taking a significant amount of risk by working with you. According to Milevsky, "This is not some large bank's money where I can write off a poor investment and go home for the weekend undamaged." own money is being flushed down the toilet." The private equity industry is made up of numerous huge firms, which garner most of the media attention; yet most private equity investments are made by thousands of small firms. Each of these courageous firms takes a risk, and any astute entrepreneur knows that this means they are asking investors to lay their wagers on their horse, their business, or their word. Private equity investors frequently take out loans to invest in businesses that they believe have the potential to expand if they are provided with additional funds, a more astute strategy, and an increase in their level of expertise. Investing is made more stressful because of this, and the investor's neck is brought dangerously near to the razor's edge of decision-making. Why should they provide money to a CEO if they perceive that the CEO has not put much of his own money at risk in his business, has not taken the time to adequately prepare for the meeting, and has the audacity to not do any research on the people he is about to meet with? Why should they? Do you think so?

They Could Lose It All with You

"Private equity is the nose of the hound dog," says Jeremy Rifkin, a futurist and author of The End of Work. Rifka believes that the groundwork is being laid for a third industrial revolution, which will be aided by this new economic framework. "Private equity is on the cutting edge of the transition." They are here because they are ready to accept the dangers. Exactly! The truth is that private equity is fantastic because of the risks it is prepared to take and the assistance it offers to company owners. Private equity invests large amounts of money but, unlike a bank, does not receive any of it back in the form of interest payments monthly within a month or two at most. They will devote their time and effort to the firm's expansion, which is another activity that the management of your local bank will not engage in. The investor had to put in a large amount of money and work before obtaining any return on their original investment or any percentage of the interest they accumulated. You must understand that, while investing in private equity may appear to be a glamorous and lucrative endeavor, the reality is that for every successful private equity investment that is cruising down the highway in triumph, there are many others that have been driven off the road and are horribly burning in the ditch. Why should it surprise you, ma'am, that people want to see the facts? They want to understand the whole financial picture. They will want to know the answers to these questions when they first hear from you. They will want these questions answered over the phone before agreeing to meet with you. When asked, "Tell us about yourself," be prepared to provide us with all this information. They do not pertain to where you were born or where you attended senior high school. The investor wants you to deliver a presentation on your firm since it shows how you sell to your customers. Keep impartiality, honesty, and authority in your field of knowledge.

Financing Mistakes Made by Rookies

Do not be fooled into thinking that luring investors is only a financial game; on the contrary, this is also a marketing game. If you make the typical mistakes made by inexperienced businesspeople, investors will show you the door as soon as they see you because it will become clear to them that you would not be a desirable business partner. If you want to do an excellent job of marketing your company to private equity investors, you need to avoid the major pitfalls that are described below.

Assuming You Are Losing Control

According to Eric Berce, managing partner at Torques Partners, "Even with a minority position, you still have power." "Since you are the Chief Executive Officer, it is up to you to make all of the operational choices and have the final word over strategy." Berce claims that when torques private equity investors pushed for Granby Steel Tanks, a company that makes storage tanks for fuel, to increase their price, the final decision rested with the CEO, and he was encouraged to make the choice. Granby Steel Tanks is a company that makes storage tanks for fuel. Customers understood that there had been no price increases for decades, so they were willing to pay the increased rates once they were put into effect.

Mistaking Private Equity for the Bank

Each individual investor in private equity agrees to shoulder the responsibility of operating near your business for the next five to seven years. While they wait for you to repay the money they invested, they are not receiving a salary commensurate with that of a banker. According to Thomson Financial, the typical amount of time an investor keeps their money in the stock of a company is six years. That is one way to put it, isn't it? This endeavor is not for those who lack a strong stomach. Instead of putting that money in the bank, why not invest it in real estate? To tell you the truth, the reason for this is that the top private equity investor eats, sleeps, and drinks the business. They are not in it for the money; they are in it for the thrill of the journey.

Not Recognizing It is a Negotiation

When you are called in for a face-to-face meeting, you are now in a negotiation scenario; it is not the time to make a sales pitch. Some CEOs make all the typical mistakes that entrepreneurs make when they are in love with their business, which is a good thing; however, they do not recognize this. If the investor has agreed to meet with you, it indicates that they are considering making an investment in your company by purchasing a stake in it. Do not provide specifics about your product currently. No! You are selling shares in your firm, and the investors are interested in the financial potential of your company; however, they are not interested in the specifics of your products. Gaining partners is the purpose of your attendance at the event, not receiving comments on the marketing plan you have developed.

Not Being a Competent CEO

If you ramble on and on about the product, it seems that you are not cut out to be a CEO. Investors want to see a leader who can carry out their goals. Companies' CEOs must show their ability to conceive on a large scale and that their businesses can endure despite the attempts of rivals with bigger resources to copy their offerings. This should reassure clients that rival firms will be unable to reclaim their business. Before you even start talking to possible investors, keep the following in mind: They have already decided that your product is the better alternative. They want to know how you intend to persuade others to purchase it and how much profit you stand to make as a result. The annals of history are littered with instances of brilliant goods and company enterprises that failed due to a failure to capture public attention or because their owners were unable to adequately manage their cash flow. Even if your firm is still in its early stages, go from being a marketer or a product developer to becoming the CEO. Product managers do not contact the financial community as much as they should. When they do, they usually stick to their area of expertise rather than speaking like a CEO and discussing financial forecasts, cash flow, or balance sheets. Product-focused executives assume that finances should be left to accountants, yet mature leaders can mentally cycle over the company's predicted financial needs while sleeping. You may be surprised to find that many company owners and executives are unaware of the elements that contribute to the growth of their firms or deplete their financial reserves. How much does it cost you to manufacture each item you sell? What is your company's EBITDA (earnings before interest, taxes, depreciation, and amortization)? Which critical ratios do you monitor? (If you haven't already, start now.) Investors want to know how many more salespeople you'll need and how much their salary will cost the firm if you want to increase revenues by a specific percentage.

Not Gathering a Team

The folks who are deeply involved are the ones that investors are placing their money on. You do not need to have famous people working for the company, nor does your entire staff have to be actively involved in the company for it to be successful. You really need to have the names and profiles of reliable people who are willing to be written into your plan and are available at a moment's notice to support your plan in person when they are asked to do so.

Not Talking about Return on Investment

It's common to hear individuals say things like "it's not about the money, yet it's about the money," which seems to make no sense at all. That implies that finance people invest in individuals like you, but if you don't know your return on investment (ROI), you're not a desirable investment, and finance people won't invest in you. It's as simple as that. Your lack of financial expertise suggests that you lack excellent management skills. You are a techie who has not taken the effort to understand that monitoring a few financial statistics is not difficult, and this shows that you have not made the effort. Simultaneously, when the investor assesses if the scale of the investment meets his personal Internal Rate of Return (IRR) objectives, he will weigh this much more than the asset's pure financial assessment. During the next five years, he will weigh his alternatives. How much room for growth does the firm have? In this aspect, the size of the market is more important than your prior performance.

An investor's internal rate of return (IRR) is the rate of growth that a project (in this example, an investment in your business) is predicted to generate. The higher this number, the more likely it is that an investor will be interested in investing in your company. This amount will also give the investor an idea of how long it will take to recoup his original investment. After taking everything into account, the investor shifts their focus to the market. He begins to think, "What is the true worth of my money at this point?" I'd like to see it between 25% and 30%. Why should I take a risk with this firm when I can invest in a fund that guarantees a 10% return? If the option with the lowest risk offers a return of 10% to 12%, I want a return of 30% since I won't have any protection in the form of equipment to sell if things go wrong. The extra money that can be made in addition to the original investment is the operation's cornerstone. What future revenues, as well as the rate of return, should investors anticipate? In a nutshell, people who have curious about two things: "How much money will I make?" and "How much am I exposed?" They will be curious about the return on investment. It is very similar to a mortgage with a 5% annual return.

Assuming the Valuation of the Business Is Just the Money

According to the words of one investor, "More so than a bank, private equity will identify a great CEO and team." If I believe in the person in charge of the company, but the company itself is having trouble succeeding or is even failing, I will make an investment and try to breathe new life into the company by contributing my time, effort, and vision. The current situation is not taken into consideration when determining the value of the company; rather, it is determined by the anticipated earnings in the future.

Not Being Clear about What You Want from Private Equity

"A key element that decreases the value of a firm is when the owner is unsure about the role that private equity will play in the company," says Peter Caressa of Ven Growth Capital Management Inc. I have some advice for company owners looking for funding, and it's the most important advice I can give: do you really want it? Be explicit, and understand that if you are not clear, a struggle will erupt between the firm's investors and the people working on the business.   6

Imagine, if you can (and you don't want to), the day you get a check for your business. You do not want to do so. That is right—a check signed by someone who is interested in your firm. You mistakenly believe it is a 10% or 75% partnership. Whatever. Choose a fi gore. It is money that may be used to help your business. How much of it do you want to see? Your business plan is gleaming, and it is right next to the cash on your desk. In the following pages, you will discover an account of the remarkable growth that was accomplished by rigorous strategic preparation and execution. It is the tale of a firm that began as a seed of an idea with a few individuals and has grown into a full oak through pain and atrocities. Excellent! Assume that this is your company's final day. Make a note of the year in your diary. Try not to panic. Nobody is going to put a gun to your head or force you to sell anything. Whatever you choose to do, it is pointless. When you have that zero-day set out and the ultimate money worth in dollars clearly determined, you are now ready to get the financing that your business needs. It may be summarized as follows: Lock the door to your office, grab a pen and paper, and jot down the exact date and technique for your leave. It may be five or 10 years in the future, and you could indicate whether you want to sell to a competitor or have your daughter take over the company. The psychological impact of having a date and a preliminary strategy will awaken you to the notion that you will need to depart your firm one day. The specifics and timing are inconsequential; what matters is that you have a date and a basic strategy. With a detailed strategy and an estimated departure date, your management team and advisers will be able to better choose a course of action.

What to Do If You Hit a Brick Wall

When a Level 3 legacy business is forced to confront the possibility that their company, in its existing form, may not be suitable for private equity, tenacity and unflinching trust will be required to see the company through the difficult times. They want to understand how to incorporate the qualities that they need into their organization to flourish. Since the financial industry is so limited, most individuals only get one chance. This suggests that a large quantity of money is ready to be invested in you at any time and that it is easily accessible. However, money may go as swiftly as the tide pushes more water ashore. Randy Pausch, a professor at Carnegie Mellon University, had an unexpected cancer diagnosis and a prognosis of just a few months to live. Pausch created the Alice program, which allows anybody to make on-screen animated figures. When he was seven, he decided to give his moving farewell speech about how one should behave oneself. "I think that when you are told no or encounter a brick wall, it is placed there to help you determine what it is that you really desire." If you are dead bent on acquiring the financing, you will need to find a way around the roadblock and investigate alternative choices. See it as a temporary roadblock rather than a definite rejection. When you hit a stalemate with a private equity firm, gently question why the fund does not see a future investment opportunity in your business. It may come as a surprise to you. It is probable that you have spent too much money on a framework rather than developing the firm. Your cautious attitude toward protecting your company's worth may signal that you are comfortable staying at Stage 2 Lifestyle and lack the intestinal fortitude to take the risks that the private equity people require of you. Kids Company was a day-care business with seven locations and a long history of stable income, but the CEO, Victoria Sepik, feared the company was too basic to attract private equity investors. Even though their expenses exceeded their income, they were successful in attracting private equity investors by establishing a five-year strategy to construct a dedicated workforce and carry out a nationwide day-care chain.

Accept That It is Oil and Water

Level 3 Legacy businesses are aware that the first step in the process of putting together a private equity relationship is to comprehend how different their perspective will be in comparison to that of the investor. When working with private equity, business owners must be aware that their investors come from all occupations, which can make maintaining healthy relationships difficult. This creative tension brings more to the table for the company than would be the case if the entrepreneur were to go it alone. To get the attention of the investor, entrepreneurs need to have a solid understanding of the differences between the two to establish a relationship with them.

• Skip the sales pitch and go straight into the financial story as your opening statement.

• Consider the rate of return on your investment

• Respect the risk that is taken by private equity and consider why they should invest in your company if you are not going to invest in it yourself.

• Be receptive to comments and suggestions, as these will provide the most insightful and forthright assessment of the company's prospects overall.

Summary Points: Achieving Mutual Understanding

1. Since it is the responsibility of private equity investors to generate investment return from the assets that they manage, the investment decision that they make will be predicated on the specifics of the company's financial situation. Companies operating at Level 3 have the understanding that the most significant benefit that private equity can bring to a partnership is improved financial capability. Companies at Level 3 are aware of the reasons why it is essential for the focus of private equity to be on financial disclosure.

2. Level 3 Legacy businesses are aware that private equity investors invest their own money in addition to money that they borrow to purchase shares of businesses that they believe have the potential to expand if they are provided with additional funding, a more astute strategy, and an increase in their level of expertise.

3. With enough time, effort, and foresight, private equity may bring a failing or struggling business back to life or give it a new lease on life.

4. The private equity partnership takes on a significant amount of risk and investing in businesses is not viewed as the opportunity to kick back and take money out of an ATM because of the level of risk involved. Even if the private equity firm is taking the same entrepreneurial risk as the company to create and build assets,

there is still a chance that they will not see any return on the time and money they have put in the venture.

5. A partnership based on private equity does not involve an employer and an employee. It is a corporate partnership with the goal of boosting the value of the company via the efforts of both parties. Companies with a Level 3 Legacy recognize this dynamic and are aware of the reasons why investors are looking for companies that are managed by mature team players that have a different skill set than the investors themselves have.

Resilience and unwavering faith will be necessary to get through the tough times, but Level 3 Legacy enterprises must face the fact that their company, in its present configuration, may not be appropriate for private equity investment. They want to learn what characteristics define a legacy firm so that they can incorporate those characteristics into their own company.

As we get to the end of Part I, the encouraging news is that you should now be getting a better grasp on how to convince private equity partners to participate in your company. You are aware of the first actions that need to be taken to demonstrate that it is to their advantage to make an investment in a person such as yourself. Adam Smith offered this piece of advice on how to get other people to work together: "Never talk to them about our own necessities but of their advantages."

When it comes to your situation, you can now demonstrate to investors that you comprehend how They are confident that the relationship will be successful and that they will benefit from having a partner who is familiar with private equity. As we are about to see, there is a unique group of investors for every size of business, and each of these groups has specific requirements that need to be fulfilled by you, the entrepreneur.

Chapter 4

THE FOOD CHAIN: MATCH YOUR BUSINESS WITH THE RIGHT INVESTORS

If you can gain an understanding of the steps involved in attracting investors and the most effective path to take, the process will be less stressful for you, and you will not have the impression that you are a small furry animal running on a treadmill. You might even arrive at a more magnificent location than you ever imagined was conceivable. For most, it is a hard slog. You should try submitting a lot of business plans to people in the financial industry who do not know who you are from Nelly. It is possible that one or two people will wish to talk. Sadly, the most common response from investors is to return the envelopes or refuse the requests made. Take into consideration the fact that every investor is given an overwhelming mountain of "opportunities" in the form of business plans, which is enough to make anyone want to bang their head against their workstation.

Spot Investors Who Fit Your Business

Herein lies the problem of assessing the investor's "mathematical fit" with respect to the size and type of the firm you manage. According to Wael Mohamed, CEO of the growing company Third Brigade, while searching for investors, it is critical to ask the following questions: "What stage of business do they invest in? What is their typical investment? What sort of returns do they aim for? And where are they in their fund's stage?" If there is no mathematical match, they will need to make an exception to invest in you. 2 You will be ahead of many other owners if you have a firm grasp of the kinds of investors who might be interested at your stage of the development curve. Finding private equity is feasible regardless of your firm's size in today's business world; however, those who can identify the stage of their company will have an easier time concentrating their search on the suitable degree of private equity. While there is some debate over where the boundary should be drawn and if venture capital is the same as private equity, the phrase "private equity" may be used to refer to any kinds of private equity investment, from seed capital through buyouts. There are many shades of gray, but all of it is privately owned money with a constant psychological underpinning, which investors share regardless of the size of the transaction. Two simple criteria can tell you if your company is mathematically fit. First and foremost, use Figure 4.1 to determine where you are on the company growth curve. The second stage is to get a preliminary estimate of how much money you need to gather. If you take the time to clearly identify these two criteria, you will be able to connect your firm with the right investors. Let us begin by examining the food chain which will assist us in determining where you are on the growth curve and who should accept your investment proposal. Excellent. Now that we are at the growth stage, you may be asking, "Because I am at the growth stage, is it feasible for us to go and meet a venture capitalist (VC) or fund manager? Should I print copies of my business plan and give them to everybody who shows an interest in them? Stop right there, people! You need to conduct some more study and preparation before you pick up the phone and call that individual. It is illegal to sell stock in your firm, and any sane investor would avoid doing business with someone who is unfamiliar with the regulations that regulate their field. Remember that the investors you meet will need to get funds for their fund somewhere, so keep that in mind. You may believe that you are the only one asking, but financing companies have also had to turn to begging in order to get funds. Private equity is basically just one giant food chain, which may surprise you. To receive funds from private equity, you must be aware of your place in the food chain, and more particularly, you must understand where you fit.

Accessing Private Equity

You might think that working in private equity is a simple career because all it entails is paying out cash to pleased business owners.

As they count their cash, investors must deal with more problems than just paper cuts. One of their biggest pet peeves is the persistent phone calls made by business owners (no, they do not back start-up airlines in Australia or ideas you had over the weekend). The plethora of jargon that is included in business plans and the excessively wordy presentations that are made in first meetings bore investors to death and make Hugo Chavez appear to be more reserved. You may make their job easier by first determining which fund is interested in your business and then constructing your message in a way that caters to the fund's specific interests. Before going into further detail, let us take a moment to go over a brief review of the distinct categories of investors. • Angel investors and seed investors invest money in young businesses that have the potential to see rapid expansion.

• Venture capitalists look for firms and individuals who have been in business for ten to eighteen years and have a history of profitability before making an investment in them.

They are going to put money into an idea.

• Growth Capital private equity will make investments in firms that have a solid foundation and a profitable track record.

• Mezzanine Capital is a form of quasi-equity in which a firm is often not required to give up any equity, although in some cases it may be required to give up a tiny amount of equity.

• Buy-out private equity is interested in purchasing existing firms with the intention of enhancing their operations. In former times, they would take over a company, then break it up and sell it off piece by piece; the action depicted in the movie Wall Street took place during this time. Private equity will, in today's market, expand and improve businesses in 99 percent of all deals.

The stage of your company, from startup, to mature corporation, will impact the amount of money you may anticipate receiving and the type of investor that will provide it. Each distinct type of investor has a one-of-a-kind risk tolerance and set of requirements for you to fulfill.

If You Are an Early Operating Company . . .

When looking at the distinct categories of private equity, an early operating company should be placed in the development capital category. This is because seed funds and angel investors know how to operate with a lower amount of capital and can help you establish the most important priorities as your business starts to expand. When you first starting out with your company, you may receive advice from others to discuss a potential opportunity with members of your own family and social circle. Love money is money given to you by those who know and care about you, such as family and friends; hence the name "love money." Their investment is often made for motives other than monetary gain; for example, your mother may want you to move out of the basement and into a more grownup lifestyle. This is the phase in which attracting investors is the least difficult, but it also has the potential to give you more worry than it is worth. When Mark Twain offered the sound advice that "Friendship will survive a whole lifetime if not asked to give money," he was speaking from experience and understood exactly what he was talking about. It would be incredibly naive of you to invest Great-Aunt Bessie's whole retirement fund in your high-risk business venture, especially when there are alternative opportunities available, such as angel investments. You can thus have peace of mind knowing that you will also always be welcome at the Thanksgiving meal with the entire family, rather than being excluded permanently from the group. There is a wide range of potential funding sources for business expansion.

Tough Angels

Consider seed investment while your company is pre-revenue, undertaking alpha testing in Saskatchewan, beta testing, or commercialization. While you are in the early stages, you have a few consumers who are paying for your concept. You could just have a prototype, but you still need to do marketing and product development. At this stage, it is reasonable to begin searching for seed funds, often known as "embryonic funds." If you are willing to fill out all the proper paperwork and wait an unusually long period for approval, you may be eligible for government assistance via the Business Development Bank of Canada (BDC). Nonetheless, the benefits are well worth the work. If you have consumers outside of Canada, contact Export Development Canada (EDC), an entity that gives financial assistance to bank loans and is innovative in its approach to financing. Because of their low profile, even your tax accountant may miss grants as a possible source of income. It is essential that you engage in the government's IRAP and SREDS tax credit programs. These schemes provide tax rebates on payroll expenses and may be useful at any stage, depending on the industry in which you operate. Examine the plethora of tax benefits provided by the government to aid in the running of small businesses. The government offers a range of financial aid in the form of grants, tax credits, and other initiatives. Financial institutions are more inclined to give credit when a loan is secured by assets like a building or an EDC. They can lend money even under adverse conditions, and some financial institutions, like HSBC, have established specialist services for company owners because they recognize that supplying this market sector is the best way for them to grow their operations. When your bank manager calls, you immediately have a horrible feeling about the day since he has a face that would make a newborn weep. You are not alone. This stomach-churning relationship with the bank starts when you are generally severely underfunded and your credit cards (American Express, Visa, and MasterCard) are all maxed out to the maximum limit to keep the business rolling. To meet the standards of most financial institutions, you may begin by dipping into your 401(k), purchasing a life insurance policy, or mortgaging your home. When you approach lenders in the future, the first thing they will ask is, "How much of your own money have you invested?" This is an intelligent question to ask since private equity investors want you to have a significant investment so that you will stay motivated. They do not want you to work at Cisco if things turn challenging, which is inevitable. But let me be clear: The Bank Is Not the First Source of Financing for Private Equity The bank is a destination for major, well-established enterprises as well as firms interested in acquiring capital assets. If your firm is backed by deposits and you have a rich partner in the business, banks may be prepared to supply you with a loan. In most circumstances, there are alternatives to the difficult and costly bank financing that is accessible, and these options will not lead your spouse to have a mental breakdown while you pursue your desire. Sleiman Breweries' proprietor, John Sleiman, was about to export his first batch of beer when his lender called his loan against the mortgage. With his mortgage, John Sleiman had secured the money. That was a terrible turn of events, but it also cost him his wife and his house. The bank did not believe beer to be a successful business. John adds, "I'm not sure why they didn't inform us sooner. I have no idea why." Sleiman, ironically, is now a publicly listed corporation on the Toronto Stock Exchange (TSX), with four breweries and yearly beer sales of 1.1 million hectoliters.

During the start-up stage, you may dream big, like Robert Deluca did when he started Porter Airlines, which flies out of Toronto Island and is only a few minutes away from downtown workplaces. Porter has successfully secured a total of $135 million to far, due in significant part to the assistance of private equity companies such as Edge stone Capital, Borealis Infrastructure, GE Asset Management, and Dan cap. Do you think you'll be able to pull it off? If you, like Deluca, have experience as a pilot and operating an airline, the answer is yes. Deluxe, at the age of fifty-six, is a successful entrepreneur with whom private equity investors have faith and with whom they are comfortable cooperating.

Seed and Start-Up

Seed funding is for your firm when it is in pre-revenue, alpha testing in Saskatchewan, beta testing, or commercialization. Seed may be used in other nations as well. When a company is in its early stages, it only has a few paying consumers for its concept. You may just have a prototype, but there is still a lot of work to be done in terms of development and marketing. This is the time to seek seed money, often known as "embryonic funds ", by some. If you are willing to complete the proper paperwork and wait a very long time for approval, the Bufunds ", Development Bank of Canada (BDC) may be able to provide you with government-backed funds. The end effect is certainly worth the effort. If you conduct business with customers outside of Canada, go to Export Development Canada (EDC), which offers financial assistance for bank loans and is forward-thinking in its financing methodology. Grants are a common source of money that is sometimes ignored, even by your tax expert. Make use of the government's IRAP and SREDS tax credit schemes, which provide tax refunds on payroll expenditures and may be available at any time depending on the sector you work in. Study the many tax benefits provided by the government to support small businesses. The government offers a broad range of financial assistance in the form of grants and tax credits.

This is quite enticing to banks if you have assets such as a building or if EDC is backing up a loan. They can lend money even in difficult situations, and some financial institutions, like HSBC, have created particular services for company owners because they recognize that this market sector is also the one in which they are most likely to see the biggest gain in income (see Appendix). When your bank manager calls, you can bet your day will turn bleak, even if he has the face of a baby crying. You are not alone never calls, you can bet your day will turn bleak, even if he has the face of a baby crying. You are not alone. Your stomach-churning connection with the bank starts when you are generally severely underfunded and have all of your credit cards — AMEX, VISA, and MasterCard — maxed up in order to keep the firm going. Most banks will want confirmation that you have adequate assets; you might begin by dipping into your 401(k), purchasing a life insurance policy, or mortgaging your home. The first question creditors will ask in the future is, "How much of your own money have you invested?" It's a fantastic question to ask since private equity investors want you to be totally involved for you to stay motivated. They don't want you to accept a job at Cisco if things go tough, since they know this will happen.

So let us be clear: It is not the bank that provides the first source of private equity funding. For big, well-established enterprises or organisations looking to purchase capital assets, the bank is the place to go. Banks may be willing to give loans to you if your new firm is collateralized by deposits and you have a rich partner. In most circumstances, there are alternatives to pricey and complicated bank financing that will not cause your spouse to have a nervous breakdown while you pursue your passion. These options can be found anywhere. As Sleiman Breweries owner John Sleiman was about to send out his first batch of beer, the lender who held his loan called it in against the mortgage. That cost him not only his house, but also, sadly, his wife. Beer was not deemed a feasible business possibility by the bank. "I don't know why they didn't inform us sooner," John is quoted as saying. Sleiman is currently a publicly listed corporation on the Toronto Stock Exchange (TSX), with four breweries and yearly beer sales of 1.1 million hectolitres. In the start-up stage, you may dream big, like Robert Deluxe did when he established Porter Airlines, which flies off Toronto Island and is just a few minutes away from downtown headquarters. Porter is well-funded, having raised a total of $135 million to far with the help of private equity firms Edge stone Capital, Borealis Infrastructure, GE Asset Management, and Dan cap. Are you capable of pulling this off? If you, like Deluxe, have a background as a pilot and have previously managed an airline, the answer is yes. Deluxe, at the age of fifty-six, is a well-seasoned businessperson in whom private equity investors have faith.

If You Are a High-Growth Company . . .

After you have proven that you have a business, that there is a product, and that people are paying for your firm but that you are not yet profitable, you have entered the domain of venture capital, abbreviated as VC. Venture capital is money invested in private firms that is often in the form of equity (offering shares or partial ownership) rather than money backed by assets. Banks, on the other hand, are unconcerned with ownership and would rather have their money in the form of a loan secured by some tangible asset. These loans are known as "asset-backed loans." Except for retail, real estate, and natural resource exploitation, venture capital invests in most businesses. Additionally, venture capital invests in your business at various stages of its life cycle, with each step reflecting a new form of investment. The term "patient capital" refers to venture capital. This is because "ventures" are businesses in their early phases of creation and expansion that have the potential to become successful in the future. If you look at the Sources of Funding, you will find that venture capital is mostly focused on start-up and early-stage firms that need between $1 million and $5 million in investment. Nonetheless, under the proper combination of conditions, large quantities of cash in the form of venture capital investment may be beneficial for organizations that are still in the early stages of development. Porter Airlines, for example, earned more than $100 million in start-up capital. The amount of cash raised in Canada for venture capital investments fluctuates from year to year, with $1.6 billion raised in 2006, a decline from $2.2 billion raised in 2005, and a high of $4.5 billion raised in 2001. There are two main qualities that distinguish venture capital from other, more conventional forms of financing. A venture capital investment is typical: 2. is meant to be a long-term investment (usually within three to eight years) that requires active participation by investors in the firms they support until they are adequately matured for disposal (via a sale, VC shares, or an initial public offering). 1. entails minority ownership or quasi-equity involvement in a private corporation (either holding common stock outright or having the ability to convert other financial instruments into common stock). 2. directly holds common stock or can convert other financial instruments into common stock. It is critical to understand that venture capital investments are active rather than passive kinds of funding. The bar has been raised, and most venture capitalists now make it a point to provide value to their investments in ways other than financial aid. This is done to help their portfolio firms achieve a greater rate of return on their investments. Active engagement is essential to achieving this aim, and most venture investors will, at the very least, demand a seat on your board of directors. While a venture capitalist invests for the long term, this does not always imply perpetually. The primary purpose of venture capitalists is to create a higher rate of return via a "liquidity event," which may be the sale of the firm to a rival, an initial public offering (IPO), or anything else that pays back the investments. Based on the exit plan, you will be able to determine where the greatest use of your time and resources will be.

First-Stage Financing: Expansion

When your company currently has a devoted customer base but wants to expand, we refer to this sort of finance as "expansion capital" or "growth capital." There will be some overlap between venture capitalists and institutional fund managers, who are in charge of managing privately held pools of cash entrusted to them by major banks and pension funds to invest in businesses. These astute fund managers invest in a broad range of companies, not simply trendy startups in the technology industry, such as traditional manufacturing and construction firms. Private equity funds may originate from several sources, including affluent company owners who have put their own money in a fund or professional fund managers who seek huge institutions for financial support to expand their fund. These venture capitalists and institutional investors want a five-year return on investment, ideally with a good profit. According to the findings of a survey of company owners done by the Technology Industries Association, the Series A round, first-round asking for $750,000 to $3 million was the hardest to fund. 4 Venture investors will be looking for "skin in the game" during the initial round of funding for your firm, which means they want to see proof that you care more about the company's success than they do. Are you up to your brows in trying to get money from every other possible source? Have you taken advantage of every government grant or loan, such as SREDs? Your firm has reached the point where traditional financial institutions will no longer cooperate with it, and the future is unclear. The venture capitalists want you to carry as much debt as possible, including a mortgage on your house, since they believe that if the fund fails, you will fail as well. If you are not employing leverage, it is fair to expect that if things go wrong, you will be able to walk away and leave the fund to bear the losses. The growth of corporate strategic investors such as Rogers and Bell is depressing the venture capital sales business. Businesses like Google, Intel, Pfizer, and Motorola realised that if they backed emerging enterprises, they could gain first rights to buy out the owners of such businesses early in the market growth process for $5 million instead of the $50 million that would have been necessary otherwise. In-house venture capital organisations are looking for businesses that provide complementary items or services that might be incorporated into their market sector. Since Bell Canada officials feel it is preferable to retain technology in its own private vault rather than on the market, the corporation has acquired a huge number of embryonic technical businesses. Moreover, a significant share of venture capital is being invested in organisations that have a strong basis but still have room for growth. Serial entrepreneur Alan McMillan believes that it is critical to understand the distinctions between the long-term orientations of venture capital and private equity. "Venture capitalists invest in ideas while working with seed firms, while bigger private equity funds prefer to engage with established organisations with dependable income streams," according to the report. According to McMillan, this is an important difference since "the tech growth narrative is not going to be gushing forth riches." The sweat equity is reinvested back into the firm. However, although the initial public offering on the stock market is the ultimate exit strategy, technology companies are more likely to be purchased by bigger technology companies in reality. These are the expectations of venture investors." Disney has acquired Club Penguin, an online social network founded by three parents in

Kelowna, British Columbia, who were worried about their children's internet use. Their parents were in Canada at the time. Disney is a Canadian corporation. They lacked an investor or business partner and had to rely on their own resources to fund their firm until it was sold. The final amount paid by Disney for the firm was $300 million. "They could have built the firm and then developed themselves much further and gone to Yahoo!, Google, or Disney for a much larger multiple," J.A. Albright's Rick Segal says. "But, if these early-stage startups that sell straight to a large company had paired with skilled VCs and private equity investors, they may have expanded the business and then sold it for a significantly greater multiple," he says. For example, prior to being bought by eBay for $1.6 billion, PayPal burned through $180 million in private equity investment and experience. It would be advantageous to work with the private equity partner for a few years before selling the company. Yet, if you capture a bird in your hand...

Types of Companies VC Investors Like or Do not Like

Venture capitalists do not provide a niche service like merchants. The eye Don't limit yourself to selling specific items, like backpacks for equestrians or scarves imported from France, because these kinds of businesses will not be successful or expand. It is possible to scale up quickly enough. They are not interested in service businesses for the same reasons, as it takes a great deal longer time to expand into those kinds of businesses. a business model like that of Deloitte Accounting that has a larger profit table than PayPal. A technology company that has developed a brand-new software application and is prepared to market, it is much simpler to expand one's business over the Internet to the global market. Additionally, there are additional opportunities to sell it to a company like Google or eBay.

If You Want to Consolidate . . .

If your company has been operational for several years and generates income (does this phrase make sense?) not required to have a profit and loss statement) and you want to grow even more, then you should consider the larger financiers are interested if you want to grow output or penetrate new markets. Investing greater sums of money, say $5 million and more, would fall under this category.

Growth Capital

The private equity fund is interested in providing financing to an established company in need of both reorganization and capitalization. These professionally managed funds are looking for the proprietor of a company that is interested in pursuing two different paths.

Option 1: The requirement for financial resources

Option 2: They desire growth but are unable to do it on their own.

For instance, to buy Dad out of the family firm, a company would take out some debt and invest 25% of its equity. Andy Burgess, the CEO of Somerset Entertainment, was in a similar scenario to that of Somerset Entertainment in that he wanted to grow the firm and required the funds to capitalize it, but he did not want to be constrained by the covenants that the banks offered.

Some company owners who run businesses that are eligible for private equity funding find out that their lifestyle businesses need to be taken more seriously to attract investors. In addition to her shares, a CEO was taking home a salary of half a million dollars each year herself. This kind of expense just cannot be justified in the context of professional cooperation. The bottom line will benefit more from having the rigor that private equity investors bring to the table. If this CEO had instead invested in the growth of the company's shares, rather than collecting such a huge compensation, her net worth would have increased significantly more over the course of five years. It is surprising how much money businesses may save by challenging the assumptions made by the current management team; having a third party with a new vision can be quite beneficial to an organization. When you reach this natural stage, at which you are forced to decide whether you want to expand or whether you want to be content with where you are, you may want to investigate Stage 2 Growth private equity. To be taken to the next level, changes must often be introduced to the investor. These changes include new management techniques, a new mode of governance (the way decisions are made), and a new structure. This is something that the CEO who was draining the company for her salary found out.

If You Are Established with Revenues . . .

You have developed into an established business with active markets. You are now prepared to have a conversation with the fund managers that invest institutional money. Fund managers are the same as venture capitalists in the sense that they are evaluating you; however, their requirements will be more complex and detailed, with a primary emphasis on the way you manage your firm. The primary distinction between venture capitalists and fund managers is that VCs are willing to take greater risks, whereas fund managers prefer investing in established businesses that generate consistent cash flow. They are not going to take a chance on a concept or your lively attitude.

Mezzanine Financing

It is possible that you are working toward a buyout or a listing on the stock market, and in either case, you will need money to "bridge" the gap until you receive your significant financial reward. You can receive what is known as bridge financing if your company has run out of money and you need to get a little bit extra runway space before you take off. It is more expensive, but it is rapid, and there is no need for assessments or other forms of due diligence because it is pure debt. However, it does not offer tax benefits. This indicates that there is some money that is only on loan to you and that it needs to be paid back according to a regular timetable as well as with interest. Because of this, the investor is granted some ownership in the company, giving them, some say over how the funds are used. Mezzanine financing can be obtained through institutional investors like Rayna Capital. These investors have specific requirements, including documented earnings and a continuous business that requires expansion. These larger agreements and management buy-out situations are what fund managers and merchant banks like HSBC and BMO are looking for to provide mezzanine financing, which is a combination of debt and equity. Fund managers like Argosy Partners and Wellington Capital are two examples of merchant banks.

Your Friendly Bank

Take note of your bank's position in the financial institution's hierarchy. Consider how far along a company's life cycle must be before banks will provide a large loan. Banks are ranked last. Nevertheless, banks are often the last place entrepreneurs believe they should go. Bankers are not nasty, but they are the most risk-averse and will only intervene after you have spent many sleepless nights worrying how you can live without losing your home and life savings. Only when you have a proven, regular clientele, fresh business, and a healthy cash flow the following are the banks' willingness to finance at this stage, banks are eager to get engaged and serve as senior lenders. The eyes are like the big brother who is first in line for dinner and can grab all the things he wants before the others even look. If anything goes wrong, they have the power to pick at your company's assets to settle their costs. To be clear, banks must safeguard their clients' money, so it is acceptable that they be more cautious in practice. "I'd want to borrow some money," you explain. How many times have you imagined your bank manager grinning like a stuffy, preserved crocodile on display at the Royal Ontario Museum at this point? True, banks seem to be lightning conductors, generating complaints from company owners, but this is due to customers being unaware of the

bank's   stance.
Even Robert Frost chimed in, stating, "A bank is a facility where they lend you an umbrella in good weather and demand it back when it starts to rain." Yes, but at the risk of repeating myself, this is a good cause. Keep in mind that banks are for senior debt financing, which means they have first dibs on any assets if your company goes bankrupt. If you want to be wise with your money, you must first understand what a bank can and cannot do. It may come as a surprise to you. The fundamental premise is that bank financing is a fantastic option if your company is low risk.

Four Differences Between Private Equity and Conventional Banks

With talks on how to tax private equity at the same rates as banks, it is worth understanding how private equity and banks work and why the private equity investor is an entrepreneur rather than a cog in the giant corporate machine.

1. Risk. Equity investors are willing to risk their entire investment but exchange that risk with the hope that the business would develop and multiply like rabbits reproducing with equally passionate rabbits. "When you put your own wealth at risk, you are an entrepreneur too. If you do not put your own cash at risk, you do not work as hard at it," says Peter Plows, the manufacturing expert with Cobalt Capital. Banks loan against real estate, automobiles, and equipment because they are fi rest in line to seize things to sell off and get back the money they loaned.

2. Long Term. Venture capital money is a long-term investment ranging from three to seven years. Bank repayments begin within months, whereas the VC payback can happen later.

3. Grow Together. The VCs and the fund managers do expect to be active in the firm and its strategy to grow. Th e VC involvement varies by fund, but they will continue sticking in the oar until the business has matured sufficiently to take public or sell or for the

owner to earn back the business. Usually, private equity investors will desire a board position. Banks may take a board seat too and advise you where they want the money spent or not spent. The diff Terence is that there is no endless upside for the bank. The loan and repayments are set and never change no matter how well you do.

4. Partners Not Lenders. The money comes with the requirement that the investor has minority or equity participation (owning common shares outright or having the right to convert other fi noncoal instruments into common shares). Psychologically, banks lend while equity partners want you to expand the business and will help you to accomplish so. Banks merely want that consistent repayment and if you grow, well excellent for you.

Know Your Way Around the Funds

As previously said, the VCs and fund managers you contact are part of the begging food chain. Pension funds and endowments contribute to venture capital funds. A venture capital fund is at the bottom of the food chain. The Eye has previously petitioned for money into their fund from large banks, corporate pension plans, and union pension plans, such as HOOPP (Hospitals of Ontario Pension Plan) and the Ontario Teachers' Pension Plan funds, by providing a particular rate of return. The VC and institutional funds are not people who have a lot of money and wish to give it away to help others. Since they must repay the money they borrowed, the eyeballs must provide a reasonable return. There are numerous non-coal expectations made by those who contribute to the fund. Individuals who will lend them money anticipate a bigger return than the average stock market return.

Institutional investors are a common source of funding for venture capital firms. The venture capitalist is a little fish vying for a slice of the financial pie. The government is also a funder, as is the Business Development Bank of Canada (BDC). The government provides the loan money. There are labor funds comprised of thousands of individuals, each of whom has invested $5,000, with the median investor being a grandmother. Corporate funds include the Dow Venture Capital Fund. These people usually come in with high expectations, only to learn that it is a long-term investment and withdraw.

If You Want the Public Market . . .

Owners want to obtain money for their challenging work and sell ownership to another company or go public with an IPO. The IPO is where you move from the private money to public money. Th e TSX-V has worked hard to create a range of options for smaller companies as well as the big IPOs:

• Capital pool,

• Reserve takes over (RTO), and

• IPO.

Sources of Funds

You will need to give some consideration to the structure of the next round of financing that you carry out. It could take the form of either a public offering or a placement in private equity. When it comes to the general consumer market, size most certainly does matter. Going public allows a company to accomplish several goals at once, including the creation of a market. There are two distinct kinds of funding available.

1. Public. A prospectus is read in its entirety. It is prohibitively expensive and well exceeds the financial means of all small firms.

2. Private. There are still regulations in place that govern how you should go about doing this and which legal stakeholders are permitted to take part.

It should be highlighted that a significant fraction of firms makes the error of going public too soon and subsequently regret it. The problem is that if a firm is insignificant, its shares are seldom traded, and there is no market for them at all. "When a firm is still small, which may be under $50 million, analysts see no reason or profitability in writing it up, and brokers don't follow it since stocks that rarely move don't pay them much fee," explains Matrix Fund Management's Roger Dent. "When a corporation is still small, which might be less than $50 million," Going public is an expensive venture; in addition to the brokers' profits, there are also the legal fees. There are the staggeringly high expenses of legal counsel and auditing services. Private placements are less costly. Also, there is a far greater degree of freedom in the contract structure. There are ongoing yearly fees in addition to the cost of getting the required funds to go public. Listing costs plus the expenditure of putting together and publishing quarterly reports, convening annual meetings, giving investor relations advice, and other similar activities will cost you at least $120,000 each year, if not more. Moreover, if your stock does not perform as well as your new shareholders expected because there is not enough of a market following for it, you may get calls from disgruntled and angry investors seeking information. If your next round of funding is estimated to be approximately $10 million, it will be large enough to attract the attention of institutional investors. You may discover that pursuing the private equity route is easier and less costly than following the standard venture capital route. According to Roger Dent, "I have no issue with public concerns as long as the time is correct."

Why Private Equity Takes Public to Private

The major private equity firms in charge of mega-deals take businesses off the public market so that they may engage in actions that induce shareholders to sell their shares or drive down the stock price. They will return the firm to the public market after they have done cleaning the house. The debate over whether private equity businesses are better off using this method than public corporations continue, although statistics are starting to demonstrate that the latter is. A recent study by Josh Lerner of Harvard Business School and Jerry Cao of Boston College examined over 500 businesses brought back to the public market by private equity firms. They discovered that the values of these firms climbed not just faster than the general indices but also faster than those of companies that were not affiliated with private equity. According to the research, if private equity businesses are held for three years or longer, their long-term performance outperforms that of public corporations by 18%. 7 Yet, the blindfolds are coming off, and activist shareholders of public businesses are beginning to demand that the management of public corporations behave similarly to public equity partners. The key shareholders of Carrefour, the world's second-biggest retailer, urged that the business operate as if it had a private equity partner, such as Blackstone or Onex. Carrefour is the world's second-biggest retailer. Because of their engagement in other activities demanding a long-term commitment, they amassed cash from the sale of real estate and invested it.

Buy-Out Financing

Business owners used to see the initial public offering (IPO) as the equivalent of conquering Mount Everest, but even finance has its trends. If the firm is listed on the stock market, it will have access to a substantial quantity of money contributed by pleased shareholders. All investors, including venture capitalists, fund managers, and management, would make a profit and then some. The situation is not always as it seems in real life, which is why it is preferable to be bought by a company established in the United States. When the Canadian business works in the same industry as the parent company, it typically demands a higher selling price, which motivates the parent company to put more cash into the subsidiary to assure its continued success. Going public is one approach to swiftly raising funds; however, investor interest may decrease after that, which is particularly common for smaller enterprises, leaving the company "orphaned." It may be tough for the CEO to get finances as well as pay the appropriate accounting costs.

Choose Your Type of Investment and Investor

You are now educated in angel investors, seed investors, venture capital, and institutional investors. You are aware of the various functions that are performed by banks, money, and other financial institutions. It is analogous to a Sudoku puzzle, however once you fill in the necessary information, the solution is shown. The rest will take care of themselves. You can see that there is a path with essential steps for each company. that both your current investors and your potential future investors will be interested in seeing. Nobody can know what the future holds for you, but they can speculate based on the significant moments in your past.

Dig for Detail

Before we move on to the subject of what we need to do to get funded, it might be worthwhile to take a quick look once more at all the possible investors who are currently out there and the requirements that they must fulfill before they will give you even one dime. There are appropriate places for bank financing and private equity when it comes to assisting you on your journey. In the following chapters, you will learn when and how to use various forms of capital, as well as how to interact with various investors. To start things off, there come the angels. Let us figure out how to get our hands on a slice of heaven, shall we? As is the case in everything else, there are good angels and bad angels, and it is imperative that you identify the good angels. The venture capitalists and, finally, the private equity fund managers are the next people on our agenda to meet with.

Chapter 5

WHAT ANGELS AND SEED FUNDS NEED

To use a metaphor, angels are the "white knights" of the economy. Without angel investors, many businesses would never make it beyond the "seed" stage. You're already aware of the eight phases of business growth and the usual investment points made by angel investors. They are best employed in the early stages of your venture if you have some experience and want to avoid using 10 credit cards to build the business. They are situated in the early phases of your enterprise. Angels are defined as "private investors" by Dan Mothersill, the guy who founded the National Angel Organization. They come from a variety of backgrounds and have worked in a variety of fields. They are enthusiastic about business and wish to inspire people to be as enthusiastic about information technology, manufacturing, alternative energy, finance, service sectors, or anything else in which they are engaged. Angel investors will provide between $250,000 and $500,000 in money, as well as their experience and the pleasure of supporting your firm. Angel investors may connect you with their wide networks, placing you in front of the right individuals to help your business grow. This is particularly critical in the early stages of a company when a lot of success is determined by whom you know.

Use Other People's Money for Early Investing

Angels are willing to take on financial risks that would cause the normal banker to run for cover in terror. Angel investors typically get engaged during the most difficult phase of a company's development, frequently before there are even a few paying customers. They are the gardeners of the early growth businesses while the businesses are still just little seeds beginning to blossom. Angel investors are eager to impart their wisdom to facilitate the rapid and sustained expansion of the enterprise.

Four Types of Angel Investors and Why They Do It

When you are near a professional investor, you will have stronger motivation to make an investment. "Can I anticipate a good return on my investment?" and "What type of return on investment can I expect?" At this stage, the funds are unsecured, indicating that there is no building to sell or mortgage to be claimed. If anything can be retrieved, the angel is incredibly lucky. Moreover, there are no recorded claims on the assets, implying that the assets are free and clear if the owner wishes to borrow money from a bank. As a result of the angel investor's engagement in the firm and the availability of financial resources, your company has a strong bank balance and no outstanding obligations. Your capacity to receive loans, frequently up to three times the amount of equity you have, will grow according to the amount of equity you have. Banks are prepared to provide you with much more money since you have invested $500,000 in the firm. The main building block of private equity is the use of debt. You should be prepared to give up a significant amount of ownership at this early stage. Angel investors need a significant stake in your company because, as your company grows, you will shift from angel investors to venture capital (VC) investors, and the angels' equity position in your company will shrink because of this change (become smaller). To demonstrate their argument, the Maple Leaf Angels present the following illustration: "If our angel group members invest $500,000 at a pre-money valuation of $1 million (and thus end up owning 33% of the company), and then a venture capital firm invests $5 million the following year at a pre-money valuation of $5 million, the original angel group investors will now own only half as much of the company, despite the fact that the company's value has more than tripled." 1 Angel investors desire between 25 and 50 percent of the fully diluted ownership in the company they invest in in order to benefit from their efforts.

1. Family Members

Your mother or another member of your family is the first angel investor or willing individual to make an investment. It is possible that your parents will hand over the money to you because they believe that "this will be good for our boy, Billy." This early equity—which may have come from an inheritance, followed by contributions from family and friends—enables a certain amount of track record.

2. Corporate Angels

The experienced angel investor will want to see evidence that the entrepreneur is serious about the business and that it is gaining sufficient traction to become something. The corporate angel is a prosperous entrepreneur who runs his own company and has around $200,000 in liquid assets at his disposal. This type of investor is often prosperous and oversees businesses with annual sales of at least $50 million. They sold their company to a large corporation such as IBM, and as a result, they are flushed with cash now. One thing you should know about these angels is that they are not yet prepared to hang up their wings and retire. They will want to take part in the action that is taking place. They are interested in working as consultants. It is possible that these potential sources of capital will need to be persuaded to invest their money in something with a higher level of risk than their current investment portfolio.

There is a possibility that certain corporate angel investors are more interested in what you can do for them than in what they can do for your company. It is possible that they are considering ways to sell your company to the very first interested buyer who comes along, in the hopes of recouping their initial investment plus a significant amount of additional funds. This variety of angel is dangerous and may at first appear to be a savior; but they may eventually transform into an Agent Smith wearing dark glasses and force you to travel down a Matrix highway in a direction that you do not choose to go. Google potential angels' past firm investments.

Are the companies still operational, and how are things doing for the people who started them? There are angels that are not immediately evident surrounding your company at this very moment. Examine the entirety of your company chain, from your customers to your suppliers, to see how you may improve the efficiency of your cash flow. You can delay payments to suppliers, whether the suppliers are aware of the situation.

3. The Retired Executive Angels

This angel seems like a successful businessperson who has since retired. They have the time and networks that you can tap into, but it is possible that they will not want to be as active in the day-to-day operations of the business. It is possible that you have hopes that they will make up for lost time and assist in expanding the consumer base or finding potential investors. They may be looking for someone to talk to because they are lonely.

Pay attention to the ratio of the amount of time they spend talking about themselves to the amount of time they spend learning about your business to avoid becoming someone who is used more for the purpose of visiting memory lane than for the purpose of growing your business. Give them a whiff of the battle of getting a business up and running, and it stirs up their blood to get back in the game without the day-to-day responsibility. They love the challenge of business, and they are old warhorses. Give them a whiff of the battle of getting a business up and running.

4. The Old Money Angels

Finally, there are the angels of old money. These are wealthy families who are interested in funding businesses. When they want to accomplish something philanthropic at the same time, they will sometimes give away money. It is possible that they desire to assist environmental causes, education initiatives in the inner city, or even their own pet interests. Bill Young, who is a family member of Bob Young, the founder of Red Hat, and who also founded and runs Social Capital Partners, has provided funding to a number of social enterprises. Social enterprises are businesses that employ disadvantaged populations such as new immigrants, single mothers, and other such groups. Turnaround Couriers is a good example of a company that helps at-risk youngsters find jobs and provides services to some of the top law firms and banks in the city. Turnaround Couriers is a bicycle courier company. If you want to improve the world by teaching people how to fish rather than providing them one philosophy, SCP can help with both funding and HR help. If you want to improve the world through teaching people how to fish rather than offering them one philosophy, contact SCP.

How to Recognize the Angel Investor

You may be shocked to find that, in addition to having a lot of money, angel investors have a lot of other characteristics. These are not the folks who belong to famous clubs or live a life of champagne excess. It is probable that they are the humblest people in middle-income communities. While some women are active, most people engaged are male. Texas is happy to have a Women's Angel Club for its citizens. Angel investors tend to gather in specific industries, such as the technology business, the biotechnology sector, or the medical device sector. Examine the numerous trade organizations. Angels will become active in their vocations by joining specialized groups and organizations. They will either make presentations or be cited in different newspapers. Google the problem in your industry, read the stories about it, and then call the interviewees. Attend industry conferences and make a point of introducing yourself to every presenter and collecting business cards from them. You should next phone them and inquire about people who are investing in your community. If these people are interested in investing in your firm, you should contact them as well. You may identify angel groups by doing a fast Google search, and their websites will detail how to approach them. Angel organizations may be found in almost every major city.

You will encounter angels in your market area. Angels appreciate being near their heavenly home. Most angel investors focus their financial assistance on businesses situated within one hundred kilometres (km) of their homes. They do not want to drive an exorbitant distance, and they most definitely do not want to fly. Many angel investors get to meet company owners via social activities, such as watching the owners' spouses participate in a tennis match. During a business breakfast, keep in mind that the person sitting next to you may be your opportunity; so, it is critical to share your company's story with others. Projects that are simple for angel investors to understand are quite appealing to them. If they have previously worked in agricultural enterprises, there is a very small chance that they will migrate into the oil and gas sector. People are typically reluctant to go into strange territory. They have prior experience working in your industry, but they are also analytical thinkers. Since they are acquainted with your industry, they can provide a bird's-eye perspective of the situation and leverage this expertise to make shrewd investments. Identify someone who has clout in the business. Identify someone you admire but are scared to approach because you respect them. People will be interested in your company. Angel investors want to invest in companies where they believe they can add value to the deal. When it comes to gaining financial assistance, you already have a leg up on the competition if you have a clear notion of how an angel investor may provide significant value to your organization.

Key Factors That Attract the Attention of Angels

If you are talking to angel investors about your company, you should be familiar with the primary criteria they look for in an investment and you should sprinkle these criteria throughout the conversation. Distance is typically the first consideration most people make. The angel investor's primary residence and the location of the business cannot be more than two hours apart. There are always going to be exceptions to the norm, but these are the exceptions.

• Interest in the Sector The information technology industry, the biotechnology industry, and the manufacturing industry are typically the most prominent, but there are other industries as well, such as firms for the web.

"Web 2.0 companies employ open-source tools, which means they require a lot less capital to construct their service," says Bryan Watson, executive director of the National Angel Organization, which is based in Toronto. In the past, Internet companies would have needed anywhere from $1 million to $2 million to get to market, but now a Web 2.0 company can get there with anywhere from $50,000 to $250,000.

• Amazing Bargains. Your business needs to be clear and straightforward. Medical equipment is an excellent product to market because it is both tangible and easy to comprehend. Because technology is typically more difficult, you will need to identify the large firms that may eventually become your target clients and investigate the possibility of networking with senior executives within those companies.

• A revenue curve shaped like a hockey stick. Angel investors put their money in early on, when the deal is at its most precarious stage, and they expect to see growth of 200%, not just 20%. Because angels are high-risk characters, these growth rates will thrill them if you can show that you are able to justify the financial figures in detail. Angels are excited about high-risk individuals.

• A Strategic Plan to Expand. If you want to become the most important item in Richmond, British Columbia, that is an admirable goal; nevertheless, the angel will not provide you with any financial assistance. You need to know most businesses are forced to conduct most of their operations outside of their comfort zone and, in modern times, outside the borders of their own country.

• Experience. Angel investors are interested in meeting business owners that have grown a startup from zero to ten million dollars in revenue. Angels place a higher value on individuals who have experience in the real world. They want to see evidence that you have that experience, and if you do not have it yourself, you will need to make connections with those who do have it. You cannot do without someone with that level of experience on your advisory board.

• An Attractive Opportunity for Financial Investment Even if your technology is the most advanced on the market, which is not what is important. Remember Beta and VHS. Beta was significantly superior, but it was shortly overtaken by VHS in popularity. Even if you have access to the most advanced technology, which does not guarantee victory. The investment proposal is necessary for you. Someone must shell out cash to get your wares. Engineers who are overly confident in their designs are at risk of suffering from myopia when it comes to commercialization.

• Capacity to Persevere. Being the first to market is no longer a desirable position. In the end, Google came into the market for search engines at a late stage. The requirement here is for long-term viability. Will you be able to compete effectively if someone enters your competitive arena with a considerable number of financial resources? You must give some thought to the best way to prevent new competitors from entering the market.

Is it possible for you to retain your customers in some way? The machines that played VHS tapes were available for a lower price compared to the BETA version's devices. Even though the quality of the product was far worse than that of VHS, the market was swayed toward the VHS side because of the price point.

• An Advantage in the Market Place. Determining what it is that sets you apart from your rivals and offers you an advantage is of the utmost importance. To have this suggests that everyone else is still using a slide rule, but you have a more advanced pocket calculator. What aspects of your offering have the potential to tilt the market in your favor? What will make your product unique if not exclusive? What will make it difficult for competitors to enter the market, catch up, and erase your name from the map?

• The Written Plan. At this early stage, it is helpful to have a business strategy that is both comprehensive and easy to understand. Angel investors will spend their time performing their own research and analysis as part of their due diligence. You will be able to assist in shortening the procedure if you have already completed the analysis of your competitors as well as all the components of looking at your organization. This will result in receiving money more quickly.

• The rate of return on the investment. Angels will demand ten to fifty times the amount of money they invested. They want evidence that you have a viable exit strategy that will allow you to buy them out of their ownership stake in the company. You will never be able to accomplish this with the money you bring in, therefore you will need a strategy to find someone who is interested in purchasing you. Keep in mind potential buyers for your company and the companies of the future.

Enter the Dragons

CBC opted to name a reality show about venture capitalists Angels' Cloud. The title "Dragons' Den," which is arguably a more appropriate description of the event, refers to the process of trial and error that entrepreneurs go through to locate angel investors. Trent Kitsch was one of the people proposing an ownership stake in his sports firm. The company that manufactures underwear is known as Sax Apparel Ltd. He makes the following claim: "I wasn't simply searching for money to invest when I initially began seeking angel equity investment for Sax; I was looking for excellent money to invest with. I've turned down offers for shares worth thousands of dollars from numerous sources. Members of my own family and friends, as well as highly affluent people who were exclusively interested in making financial investments in my firm, were among those who expressed interest. I assumed that the most effective way to pursue me for the seed round of funding would be to approach individuals in the field who had relevant expertise and relationships. This strategy was unquestionably effective. My duty of requesting funds has gotten more difficult due to a limited pool of contributors and investors, but it has increased tremendously as I have met amazing, knowledgeable money angels from the field. made my first investment round far more advantageous than simply the amount of money that was collected."

Angels Compared to Venture Capitalists

Both angel investors and venture capitalists like being involved in decision-making; nevertheless, it is vital to note that angel investors choose to invest, while venture capitalists are forced to do so. As a result, their involvement in the company's management will take on a new and distinct viewpoint. To decrease the amount of pain felt after the deal is completed, it is critical to take great care in calculating the right value of the investment and to have heated dialogues early on. Examine the investor's degree of reality about the partnership's proportion. What proportion of the firm will you have to sell in order for the investment to be profitable?

Expectations about value must be controlled. "Divide the planned funding ($500K) by the provided percentage (20%) to obtain the post-money value ($2.5 million). Then deduct the money ($500,000) from the post-money appraisal ($2.5 million) to arrive at the pre-money valuation ($2 million)." According to the Maple Leaf angel group, Angel investors are quick to point out that a valuation of more than $2 million in the early stages of a company's growth is quite unusual. It is conceivable (and even advised) to employ appraisers; nevertheless, bear in mind that the most important aspect is the investor's readiness to pay. Trent Kitsch, a Sax member, concurred that "I was far wrong on my early assessments of Sax." Angel investors are like you and me when we go car shopping. There is no distinction between us. Investors were not interested in Sax when it had a post-money value of $3,000,000 and requested $300,000 for 10% ownership, but interest increased when I simply told myself, "This is a million-dollar concept!" and priced it at a post-money valuation of $1,000,000 and 10% for $100,000. Sax is already attracting the attention of investors. So, what precisely happened? We got a flood of interest at that price, prompting us to set the price of our first round of investment money at $2,000,000, or 10% for $200,000. Kitsch suggests that "the moral of the tale is to use an initial selling price of the firm's worth that is within the realm of reality or even a touch low and angels appear to come out of their shells." To continue with the car example, I may not be interested in buying a Porsche at the asking price, but I will pay attention to the salesman if he is giving me a good deal or is being honest about the cost. Sax is run by Kitsch out of Kelowna, British Columbia. In terms of public relations, his presence on "Dragons' Den" was well worth the expenditure. Kitsch's patience with dragon breath was rewarded when Sax's business plan was chosen as the best in the CBC's online competition for the best idea. Kitsch took home a $50,000 prize.

Three Don'ts When Dealing with Angels

To begin, avoid the rookie error of demanding a non-disclosure agreement; this instantly brands you as inexperienced. Angels have been where you are and do not want to be there again; they would much prefer to be an overseer as opposed to accepting your notion and beginning from nothing. Angels have been where you are today and don't want to go back. Second, if possible, avoid the urge to agree to all of their terms right away. Do you simply offer away your wares to everyone who asks? The angel would expect you to battle for the price point on your goods and would not expect to obtain what they want from you in an easy way. They are addicted to a good challenge! Trent Kitsch had this to say about it: "Never get too thrilled till the ink is dry." As I was presenting to a number of angel investors, I let my emotions get the best of me and convinced myself that I had a deal. Even going so far as to let unproven business transactions impact how I connect with other possible investors. Allowing the angels too much power over your body and emotions should be avoided unless some paperwork indicating an agreement or an expression of interest subject to points has been signed. Do not expect the angel to instantly inject the business with income; you will still be expected to undertake all of the difficult work. Finally, don't expect the angel to miraculously pump income into the firm. Indeed, a lot of company owners are frustrated with the angel investor's inability to make direct phone calls to potential customers. Explain both of your responsibilities as well as the future monthly framework. It is good to lay out your expectations for the connection and then ask the angel to read them and assess if they are met. "I operate a firm that produces Web sites for rock musicians, and I have learned to weed through angel investors who are there for the cool element rather than helping me expand the revenues," says Kevin Level, CEO of Official Community and manager of Web sites such as Blue Rodeo. "I have learned to weed through angel investors who are there for the cool aspect in order to assist me raise the revenues," Level is quoted as saying. You have much too much on your plate to waste time on pointless chit-chat at meaningless board meetings. Make a plan for the future year as well as a plan for frequent meetings. Sort the session themes into one of two categories: operations or strategy. My board and I are both conscious of our different obligations, and although I value their great knowledge of my industry and the support they give in opening doors, it is my responsibility to make the sales calls.

Types of Seed Stage Investors

After the first investment from angel investors, it is now time to pass the hat once again. You are now ready to meet with the seed fund investors. This is the first round of the dance competition, and it is really challenging. You cannot expect to be engaged in the transaction structuring or risk management processes. If things do not go as planned, the initial investor will be left with little more than some IKEA furniture and a few computers. Zip! Even patents on privately produced technology are no longer valuable. When the term sheet for the transaction has forty pages of downsized structure, seed investors are aware that they are dealing with a terrible prospect. Instead, you should focus on the company's growth and opportunities.

In comparison to the US, the proportion of total venture capital invested in seed enterprises in Canada varies from 10% to 15%, which is not a bad figure. In 2006, 51,000 enterprises in the United States got angel financing, with the average amount raised being $500,000. The software sector received the most financing (18%), followed by biotechnology (18%) and healthcare services and medical devices and equipment (21%). Remember that venture investors have seen hundreds of different entrepreneurs and categorize them as follows:

• Academic Subsidiaries and Associated Businesses Based on your business plan, you were awarded the best new company concept. You've reached the stage where you want to make things happen in the real world. Your hurdles will include an inexperienced management team and minimal market validation for your proposal. By doing a trial run of your concept or even receiving letters of recommendation from large clients, you will create a lot earlier interest in it.

• First-time participants These are the employees that were let go by Nortel. • Second-timers They are often engineers or product specialists who appreciate working with a board of directors but may find that portion of the job tough. These entrepreneurs have accomplished the first round of acquiring money and have returned for extra guidance and supplies. The eyes need less labor than the newer categories. Investors will be more sceptical at this point since business, like Hollywood, is a harsh profession; yesterday's heroes are not often today's stars.

Quick Test for VC Money

After the first investment from angel investors, it is now time to pass the hat once again. You are now ready to meet with the seed fund investors. This is the first round of the dance competition, and it is really challenging. You cannot expect to be engaged in the transaction structuring or risk management processes. If things do not go as planned, the initial investor will be left with little more than some IKEA furniture and a few computers. Zip! Even patents on privately produced technology are no longer valuable. When the term sheet for the transaction has forty pages of downsized structure, seed investors are aware that they are dealing with a terrible prospect. Instead, you should focus on the company's growth   and   opportunities.
In comparison to the US, the proportion of total venture capital invested in seed enterprises in Canada varies from 10% to 15%, which is not a bad figure. In 2006, 51,000 enterprises in the United States got angel financing, with the average amount raised being $500,000. The software sector received the most financing (18%), followed by biotechnology (18%) and healthcare services and medical devices and equipment (21%). Remember that venture investors have seen hundreds of different entrepreneurs and categorize them as follows:

• Academic Subsidiaries and Associated Businesses Based on your business plan, you were awarded the best new company concept. You've reached the stage where you want to make things happen in the real world. Your hurdles will include an inexperienced management team and minimal market validation for your proposal. By doing a trial run of your concept or even receiving letters of recommendation from large clients, you will create a lot earlier interest in it.

• First-time participants These are the employees that were let go by Nortel. • Second-timers They are often engineers or product specialists who appreciate working with a board of directors but may find that portion of the job tough. These entrepreneurs have accomplished the first round of acquiring money and have returned for extra guidance and supplies. The eyes need less labor than the newer categories. Investors will be more sceptical at this point since business, like Hollywood, is a harsh profession; yesterday's heroes are not often today's stars.

Chapter 6

WHAT YOU SHOULD KNOW ABOUT VENTURE CAPITALISTS

In the mining business, when prospectors or geologists fi Nd something that looks like gold, they will rub a touchstone across the ore. This ceramic stone helps determine whether the rock is real or just fool's gold and is an invaluable tool for determining the worth of a mineral sample. Investors, too, have their unique touchstones that they utilize for testing your abilities.

"I am often asked what Secret VC Toolkit helps us determine where to invest," venture capitalist Rick Segal of JLA Ventures, says with a smile. "Some folks claim the Ouija-board strategy works well." If you know what the investor will be assessing, you can prepare. To get inside the headspace of a hyper-intellectual and fussy venture capitalist (VC) investor, let us fi Nd out who they are, what their challenges are, and what motivates them to put their cash in your organization.

What You Need to Know about Venture Capitalists

"Private equity firms see themselves as smart, serial monogamists, constantly on the search for profitable, long-term relationships,"1 contends Daniel Gross, Slate magazine's business correspondent. A private equity investor, like a venture capitalist, seeks long-term relationships. The fundamental distinction, Terence, is where these two types of investors are located on a company's development curve fund managers are at the mature end, while VCs are between the startup and established phases. While venture capitalists may believe themselves to be private equity fund managers, they have a far higher stomach for risk and are typically more entrepreneurial, that is, impulsive, loud, and able to sum up your talents in a second. Since they are investing in you and your company, they must keep their eyes peeled.

It is a highly different event for the fund manager, who has the firm's long-term history to assess; success does not depend totally on the people in the business or on the possibilities for technological progress. If you are an early-stage company, your first step should be to send your business plan to the appropriate VC. But first, let us study because they are attracted to dangerous individuals like you.

It Always Goes Back to the Relationship

"The professional investor's basic nature is not as trusting as the company owner's," explains VC Ilse Treurnicht, President and CEO of Toronto-based Prim axis Technologies Ventures Ltd., which has since become The Mars Centre. "He is asking, 'How can this business go wrong? How would this company's owner handle me if something went wrong? Will it all come down to lawyers?'" 2

When the company owner sees a half-full glass, the VC sees a frustratingly half-empty glass; instead of recognizing potential, he or she is primarily concerned with what may go wrong. Such a negative focus may leave businesses confused and unhappy. Remember, when it comes to attitude, the answer to the question "Is the glass half full or half empty?" is "It depends on whether you're pouring or drinking!" True, the perception that the VC is the Doubting Thomas of the business world might irritate the entrepreneur, especially when this downer guy is the one determining whether or not to invest in the company idea. It is preferable for you, the CEO, to realize from the start that the sort of personality drawn to investing is an analytical beast. Few entrepreneurs would characterize their talents as "analytical," preferring phrases like "fast development of concept to market" or "put something out there and see if it sticks," while you favor Tom Peters' "Ready, Fire, Aim" approach, author of In Search of Excellence and management expert. The essence of the connection is here: creative tension. That will strengthen the company. The angel investor may be a combination of nit-picky analytical and entrepreneurial energy, but VC and institutional fund management, like the Tower of Pisa, leans more towards the nit-picky. The VC appreciates your colorful personality, but you must also utilize your emotional quotient (EQ) and accept the VC's Excel-dominated intellect. A start-up VC envisions himself collaborating with an entrepreneur to establish a business. Venture funding is a risky industry, whether at an early stage or prior to an initial public offering (IPO). Exceptional entrepreneurs think that they can change the world. The act is forceful and intoxicating. You, as the company owner, must keep this big picture in mind because you will need it. It takes a long time to get wealthy. Failure should not be feared by forward-thinking business owners. Fund managers are aware of this, but they must also ensure that you are not just sipping Kool-Aid and spreading a sugar high of incorrect assumptions.

What Do Professional Investors Expect?

Consider a nest. It can hold 10 eggs, and the mother goose waits patiently for each of them to hatch. She hopes her goslings will develop into healthy geese and ultimately fly out to build their own nests. Ideally, a couple of eggs will be golden and bring you great fortune. Fund managers also have up to ten assets that they wish to develop for five years before leaving the fund. Big funds that invest money into a VC fund expect to earn more than they would in the general market or anywhere else, putting pressure on the VC to find potentially profitable firms. "Well, my firm has sales, but not at the 25% level," you may think. Do you believe you must be profitable, and if not, do you believe the VC path is closed? There is good news. If you have money flooding in, it is quite probable that some VCs will be interested.

Your Full Dedication

Venture capitalists need to be exceedingly careful about the type of firm they pick to put into their fund. When you think that each fund may invest in ten companies, there is not a lot of room to purchase into a business that is not going to do what it claims. As your firm grows, there are several expert investors out there interested in working with you, even with all the associated dangers.

As we discussed before, nothing comes for free, and if you want capital, then VCs will want to purchase an equity part in your company. The size of their investment will be in proportion to the value of your business. Once your "skin in the game" is clear, the VCs will demand smart management, product validation, channel build-up, a rounding-out of your offerings, and an established sales force. As your firm grows and you move on from the research and development (R&D) stage, the valuation of your business will improve. The VCs like to do rollouts of the product, not merely remain in the R&D stage. The eye will want to stay around and invest in second rounds.

What Venture Capitalists Need to See Before They Trust You

There are two tasks that venture capitalists need to perform exceptionally effectively. Primarily, they must have an idea of how sizable your potential market maybe if all went according to plan. Second, they need to evaluate the capabilities and aspirations of the team. Imagine you were to meet a younger version of Richard Branson. Would you have been able to look past his hippy ways and see the steely sparkle of his dogged determination?

Job 1: Identify the Killer Weapon for Success

Finally, the venture investor wants to know the potential size of the pie. This is the market's true size, and venture investors are hunting for mega-markets. Since the firm anticipated that catering to a market of that size would be lucrative, Facebook's first target audience was college students. Alan McMillan, a successful entrepreneur who has founded many businesses, adds with a chuckle that venture investors like utilizing pie charts. "There are entrepreneurs who are disappointed that their story did not result in a larger pie, but in the end, funding from private equity may give you your greatest shot at development." The pie chart shows that it is advantageous to give up ownership to get a greater market share. This is because if your firm is provided with financing to execute all the initiatives necessary to obtain a greater market share, the value of its smaller portion of the pie will grow. Many company owners are unaware that if they borrow money to grow the pie, they will have to give up some control. Consider this before you feel enraged because people are selfish and refuse to acknowledge the truth of the situation. That it is better to have a tiny proportion of a big pie rather than a hundred percent of a crumb to eat. According to a new study, an entrepreneur who gives up more stock to attract investors builds a richer firm than one who gives up less, and even a smaller chunk at the start of the VC investment phase ends up being worth more. This discovery is even more fascinating since it shows that an entrepreneur who gives up less stock in order to attract investors produces a worse firm. According to Noam Wasserman, a researcher, most individuals who start their own enterprises want to "earn a lot of money and run the show." "New research has indicated that balancing the two may be difficult." Moreover, Wasserman warns the company's founders, stating, "If you don't find out which means more to you, you could end up neither wealthy nor king." When you decide you want to be affluent, giving up a slice of pie seems like a more appealing alternative.

What Are the Risks to Achieving Market Size?

Confronting unpredictability helps alleviate the worry that you are a short-sighted businessperson who has a massive blind spot and no backup plans.

• Technology. Those pitches that are focused on technology have a much lower chance of being successful and cause equity investors to put their checkbooks away more quickly than school children who put their books away on a Friday afternoon. According to Mark McQueen, who works at Wellington Financial, "people have blinders about their work when they sit in the basement and think they are changing the world with their new software." If your idea can be stolen during a cocktail party, then it is not worth very much, according to the viewpoint of a venture capitalist.

• The Risk of the Intensity of Industry. Venture capitalists look for industries that are expanding and teams who have the Machiavellian efficiency to exploit a certain market niche when making investments. If there are already three huge incumbents who dominate the business, would anyone notice you? Which regulations create the most hurdles? This will not be considered as a favorable opportunity if there is only one corporation that controls the entire industry. If the rock face is appealing, then other people should be there too.

• Routes to the Exits. Make a list of the ways to get out of here. Have you given any thought to what will happen to the fund five years from now and how it will make a profit on its investment while also recouping its initial investment? Have you compiled a list of prospective customers that are able to pay? Is it possible for you to collaborate with a rival business or an international corporation that has its sights set on the North American market? Also, which of your competitors could you buy to expand your business?

Job 2: VCs Must Identify a Team of Tigers

After assessing that their portion of the pie has the potential to grow, venture investors must choose the best team to work with. "Management is the key to venture capital value," says Peter Caressa of Ven Growth Management. "Until your first company fails, you'll claim it's all about management, but you don't truly understand what it means," the business owner said. "Until your first business fails, you'll think it's all about the money." Yet, if your investment does not go as expected, you will learn just how important management is to the enterprise's success. To have the investing community designate your transaction "Deal of the Year" is the greatest praise that can be awarded. Sand Grape, a company that manufactures technology to help internet service providers manage the massive amount of traffic on networks, won the award for the best business in 2007. It was funded by BDC Venture Capital, Celtic House, Tech Capital Partners, and Ven Growth, and the deal's market valuation of $600 million demonstrated its significance in the world of venture capital. As a consequence, to better grasp how to thrive in this market, consider how the venture capitalists caught and landed this fish. As Celtic House's Michael Whatman reflects on how he chose Sand Grape, he relates the tale of George Washington's early venture capital investment. A twenty-one-year-old man named Henry Knox contacted Washington with a proposition in the autumn of 1775, and Washington was one of the first persons to engage in venture capital.

Henry Knox notified George Washington that the British soldiers were securely stationed in Boston and showed no indications of evacuating, necessitating a change in the battle odds. Knox requested that he and his forces march to Fort Ticonderoga, the site of a previous military conflict in which the British were beaten and forced out, leaving a significant amount of ordnance behind. Knox set an ambitious objective of bringing all fifty-nine guns back to Boston, which would entail lugging sixty metric tons of artillery across 300 miles of frozen lakes and rivers. All of this happened back when neither a Mack truck nor a forklift were widely accessible. Notwithstanding the fact that it was impossible, Washington granted Knox permission to return the large cannons to Boston. "I have great trust in you, Henry Knox. You've done a fantastic job leading your troops, and I have trust in your capacity to solve problems. This is your money." Later, Washington would marvel at Knox's courage in enduring the winter ice while keeping his troops engaged and pleased, which is the hardest challenge for military commanders to overcome. As men working for Henry Knox tried to transport the guns over the icy river, the heaviest cannon broke through the ice. Most people would say, "Oh my gosh, just leave it behind." The gang, on the other hand, was resolute about not giving up. They dove into the icy water without wetsuits, looped a rope around the cannon, pulled it to the surface, and then resumed their journey to Boston.

By this time, Washington was certain that Knox had died of dysentery or been murdered, and he had written off his investment, as is the unpleasant requirement of any venture investor. Knox's prompt arrival made Washington very delighted since it enabled him to position weapons on the hill overlooking Boston. When the light rose, the Brits were able to see the fatal weaponry aimed at them. According to reports, their commander, General Howe, said of the rebels, "The rebels accomplished more in one night than my whole force would have done in one month." When the Brits realized they were vulnerable to a lethal attack, they promptly abandoned Boston without a fight and sailed away. Why did George Washington place a higher value on Henry Knox and his great vision than on the advice of his other generals? This is the most crucial question in the venture capital sector. In terms of technology, who are today's Henry Knox equivalents? What are their goals, and where can they discover the wealth hidden in the hills? Will they be able to rally enough people to bring that gold back, even if there's a chance it'll be lost in the ice? In contrast to so many others, Henry Knox's success may be traced to his inherently commendable characteristic of cheerfully assuming the responsibility of seeing the task through to completion. "As soon as a CEO entrepreneur says things like, 'We missed our target because our suppliers let us down" or 'I couldn't find the right people,' then I know for sure that this is not an entrepreneur I'd invest in," says Mike Volker of WUTIF Capital, a director at Simon Fraser University, and an angel investor with RIM. "They just lack the necessary skills."

People Risk

Having ideas is not hard. The actual doing is difficult. On the battlefield of business, instead of killing people, we now target and destroy firms. The squad needs to be able to switch tactics and replace the leader if any of those becomes required, but they also need to have the grit to keep going. Peter Caressa, a partner of Ven Growth Capital Management Inc., is quoted as saying, "Acceptance of mediocrity is the death knell." "You cannot allow yourself to be satisfied with being good enough. You must come out on top no matter what. When I worked at Microsoft, every department followed that attitude, and as a result, they completely dominated the industry.

Consider your own answers to these questions.

• Is there a broad perspective?

• What do you hope to accomplish with your company?

• What are the founders' goals for the company?

• Do members of the team and partners interact with one another in a friendly manner?

• Are you mentored? Who is it that is offering you guidance?

• Do you have any experience putting a strategy into action?

• How do you plan to conduct yourself when you have a board of directors watching your every move?

VCs Like Repeat Teams

Every venture investor desires the team that successfully launches one business and then starts another that achieves even more success. This is known as the "alumni phenomenon," and the history of PayPal is the most well-known example. PayPal was a roller coaster ride for the private equity partners that invested because the business's founders signed up millions of subscribers but burned through $180 million in venture capital investment before breaking even and achieving their exit plan of being purchased by a major corporation. During the dotcom nuclear winter of 2002, eBay spent $1.5 billion to purchase PayPal. This transaction occurred. At this point, the two PayPal founders could have retired and made their own film titled My Great Exit from My Start-Up Business, but they went on to reach much higher levels of success in their careers. These are the management teams that don't even have to open their eyes to get venture capital investment.

PayPal's founding team is a Who's Who of private equity transactions, including names like Facebook, YouTube, LinkedIn, Slide, Sequoia (a significant venture capital company), and charities. Venture investors understand that difficult times are perfect for learning critical lessons, one of which is that the original thought may not be the best idea. Sand Vine's initial market was the incorrect one, and the firm had a few years of flatlined income and financing requests. This is similar to the many concepts produced by PayPal alumni (YouTube was initially a dating site). The brave venture investors who were able to inject funds were the ones that persevered to attain success. According to Chad Hurley, a PayPal alum and co-founder of YouTube, which was ultimately purchased by Google for $1.6 billion, "You never think it could happen to you." Yet, witnessing Peter, Max, and the other folks (back in PayPal) generate ideas and understand how to make things work provided me with a wealth of knowledge. You may not have a business degree, but you understand how to make the process go smoothly. Because of the information I acquired from this experience, my engagement in a start-up firm is beginning   to   pay   off.
The Sandvine team created Instream, which they eventually sold to Cisco for 450 million dollars. Both the September 11 terrorist attacks and the accompanying economic collapse happened within the same month. Cisco, being the incredibly well-managed company that it is, reacted to the economic slump by making drastic and quick cutbacks, resulting in the former Instream team being laid off and granted their freedom. Andrew Whatman, a Celtic House employee, contacted David Caputo and said, "Dave, you're coming off a great success selling to Cisco. This is a once-in-a-lifetime chance to fund a competent club." You can earn money for your team right now. Whatman advised Caputo to save enough money to cross the hazardous desert that lay ahead. Even though they lacked a concept, a PowerPoint presentation, and a business plan, they were able to raise $20 million entirely on the strength of their team. The team's demonstrated track record of success in the past was the major basis for the venture investors' investment. After that, the group focused on deciding which markets to approach, and their initial decision did not prove to be the beachhead that enabled them to break through to their big

market success. The sand vine had to come to a halt and modify its route. They fell short of their projected targets, prompting numerous venture funders to discontinue their support. At this point, many entrepreneurs are angry with the venture capital industry, as a chasm opens up in front of them. This is the essence of free business, and therefore, there are many broken glasses from shattered enterprises that did not succeed, as well as from the investors who backed them. Yet, free enterprise has had a lot of success. People are injured and left with scars. When venture investors are burned, they don't forget, and they typically take it out on succeeding entrepreneurs. Moreover, some venture capitalists operate like quasi-bankers, forgetting that even when they are sitting on a pile of gold, there are still human dynamics at work. People will give you the money you need to invest if you make them laugh with your jokes about venture capitalists. When a company's revenue rises, so does the demand to get finance for its activities. Surprisingly, as the firm starts making enough money to take a step back, the tables soon flip, and venture investors want to give them money. When this happens, the entrepreneur may look back and remember which venture investors were helpful with their time and which attended board meetings despite making no contributions to the firm. Your turn will come in due course. When you eventually succeed, have the courtesy to put yourself in the shoes of your supporters. Would you have been ready to offer yourself more money if you hadn't yet attained your objectives and things weren't looking good?

What Companies Do VCs Like?

Do venture investors discover that the excellent due diligence conducted on the facts was what made the difference when they explore the history of a successful business, such as Sandvine, which earned the CVCA award for Deal of the Year? It is more probable that the quality of the team distinguished itself from the rest of the chaff; it was not only the founder alone but a team capable of operating at the required high-stress pace. What is the definition of value? Your discussion may begin with the investor asking for a short overview of your financial situation, but low

119

earnings before interest, taxes, depreciation, and amortization (EBITDA) will not put a stop to it. The fund's value, as well as the kinds of firms currently in its portfolio, affect a company's valuation. We are unable to use these indicators as value markers since many of the firms that interest us do not have EBIDTA or sales. According to Peter Caressa of Ven Growth Capital Management Inc., his team places a higher value on companies that have the following characteristics: high barriers to entry; rapid revenue growth capability; an analysis of what will happen in the market over the next three years; identification of the number one challenge to overcome; and the perfect intersection of company, services, and products with the market cycle. The investment process is riddled with intricacy and volatility. As compared to investments in other sorts of companies, venture investors in the sector of information technology understand that, in the end, everything depends on the team that is working on the project. While tech VCs may do the hard science of due diligence, research the market, and contact prior clients, the only actual metadata worth diving into is people. Predicting who will win is a far more difficult skill to master. While investing in a well-rehearsed team is a solid indicator of success, obtaining that accomplishment remains something of an art.

How to Get the VC to Call

There are certain things, such as resumes, that catch the eye of seasoned pros and get them to pick up the phone and call you. One of these things is a potential employer's interest in working with you. People, not technologies or markets, are the focus of venture capitalists' investments. It can be awful if people-related things go wrong. In the process of conducting their due diligence on you, they are also attempting to determine the kind of person you are. It is a social experiment to see what makes you click and whether you will be cooperative or will crack when you pitch in, and it is an opportunity to learn what makes you tick.

Finding a referral to a business partner is the most effective activity you can take; therefore, you should focus on doing that. It is like going on a date. They will take your call if you have been referred to a venture capitalist by someone they see as trustworthy. Poor etiquette on the phone should immediately raise a red flag. The VC is aware that they are about to begin a relationship that will last for seven years, therefore they will not spend their time with someone who annoys them. If they cannot picture themselves being married to you, they will politely decline your proposal with a "thank you, but no thanks."

Plan Well

You should budget at least a couple of weeks for preparation before meeting with a smart investor. If that does not happen, you are finished before you even begin. If you do not put in the effort, you might as well just climb into a coffee shop, throw the investor a stake, and ask them to "drive it in, please." Your business plan, which is comparable to a résumé, is the key to moving on to the next stage, which is an in-person meeting with a potential investor or client. If you can demonstrate both your vision for the company and how you intend to turn that vision into reality, it will be much simpler for you to attract financial backing for your enterprise. If you have a merger possibility on the horizon that you can name, you can make yourself a lot more appealing to potential investors in your company. According to Treurnicht, investors are more interested in the people behind the product than in the product itself. "And if rest impressions are essential. Maintain an active interest in the topic at hand while avoiding arrogance. Because a relationship with a bank or venture capital firm might last anywhere from four to eight years on average, investors look for people they like and think they will have a good relationship with.

The VC Screening Process

Deals that are presented to venture capitalists must first be evaluated. You must stand out among the thousands of other ideas that they review to grab their attention. Your business strategy may or may not be able to assist you differentiate yourself from the competition. Forget about it if you do not have a good plan to begin with.

Where Does Your Deal Fit?

Ask your venture capitalist about the possibility of placing your company's investment within their fund's horizon. If your company was the first to join, you will have an extra five years to increase your sales before you must return the original investment in full. If you arrive last, the VC's window of opportunity to flee will be narrower. When you meet with venture capitalists and where they are in the creation of their fund are other key factors to consider. If they have already invested most of their wealth, they will be highly selective in the remaining two enterprises in which they invest. If they have just recently received the money, they are more likely to give it away. Find out who will be managing your case once you've made the investment. Will it be the same person who did the background check and spent time getting to know your company? Such a person will develop an emotional connection to the cause. You can anticipate a lot less devotion from a new face working on your case. The venture capitalist is a creature with a high potential payoff for a high possible risk. Three out of every ten firms in their fund will drive the fund's return. If your firm is in that portfolio and is struggling, you might expect some pressure from the venture investors. They want winners because they make the most money from them. Venture capital (VC) investors make money for the individuals who make them money. Their usual life cycle is ten years: the first five years are spent sowing the seeds for your business, and the next five years are spent enjoying the fruits of your investment. It is critical that the VCs flee. They are not there to help you with your retirement finances. The venture investors understand that they would have to invest their own time in completing due diligence on the firm. They have a responsibility to research your company and evaluate whether or not what you claim is true. Have you attempted to depict your organization and the risks involved with it, or have you hidden a few issues that might result in a five-lane pileup in the future? Venture capitalists will have many questions, but according to Adam Breslin of Pender Management, "part of the process is to come to grips with the risks and establish a degree of understanding between the entrepreneur and the investor as to what the risks are and how to try to avoid the holes."

Risks to Watch For

"The hazards that company owners confront in today's environment are so much more complex than the core challenges you envisioned at the beginning to sell your product to the market," according to Breslin. The risk list is so overwhelming that many company owners prefer to ignore the majority of these threats   entirely.
Most company owners, according to CEOs, have a natural aversion to risk management. That looks to be just another set of authoritarian constraints meant to deflect their focus away from their primary goal, which is to raise income. Breslin observes in his paper that "the more CEOs accept the obstacles they face, the more they grasp that an active, integrated approach to risk management will really pay off, and frequently sooner rather than later."
The following are some of the risks highlighted by investors and CEOs, as well as some of the remedies provided by them.
• Strategic danger These are the possible losses that might result from making bad strategic resource decisions. Your risk profile is determined by the goods and services you choose to provide to carefully selected markets. The sale of books produced by the Toronto-based firm Shore Publishing and its chief executive officer, Penny Shore, bears the highest danger, for example. According to Shore, realizing her organization's vulnerability motivated it to reduce its risks by transitioning from the volatile business-to-consumer publishing sector to the more stable business-to-business publishing market.

• The risk of operational failure Internal processes, people, or system failures, as well as the occurrence of external events, may all result in operational risks. When things don't go as planned, company owners typically realize the importance of seemingly small activities for the first time. The SARS epidemic in Toronto in 2003 was widely publicized across the globe. Desert Spring Products, based in Mississauga, has customers in both Asia and Europe, according to Peter Vanderlin, Chief Executive Officer. The success of the company's main product, an innovative indoor humidifier, is dependent on its sales representatives and distributors completing an important training program. As SARS became publicly known, marketing employees in the United Kingdom refused to work with their Canadian colleagues. "That almost shut down our activities," Vanderlin says. The repercussions lasted more than a year. We will be more prepared the next time since we are aware that this is an important part of our sales process.

• Security risks to the information system This puts you in danger of losing control of personal customer data in an age when privacy regulation is becoming more important. Sam Dennis, CEO of Radium Canada, a digital advertising firm located in Toronto, said that although most of his business is performed in Canada, he is needed to keep up with the constantly changing legislation in the United States. This is due to the fact that the majority of his clientele are Americans, yet the privacy rules will still apply inside Canada. He may find himself unable to comply with Canadian legislation while in the United States.

• The Risks of Outsourcing This term refers to losses caused directly by interruptions in the services provided by multiple providers. The hazards come when outsourcing portions of a medical device, for example, to manufacturers that do not comply with your firm's quality and behavioral requirements, according to Arun Megawatt, CEO of Nevada Technologies, a publicly listed company located in Mississauga that manufactures medical devices. Parts of the medical gadget in issue are outsourced in this case. Megawatt claims to be very careful when examining suppliers and the dangers they pose. "When it comes to medical equipment, you're dealing with patient safety issues as well as legislation that has a huge impact."

• Threat to security When a company loses assets, cash, or accounting information, there is a security risk involved. This is an excellent example of how paying attention to risk can help, rather than hurt, your bottom line. According to Jack Hoang, CEO of i3DVR, his business has created software that can count the number of customers queuing in front of a restaurant counter. The system will then be able to anticipate revenues in real time and show any abnormalities, discouraging counter personnel from trying to steal any money.

• Legal Danger This kind of risk includes losses caused by a breach of the law or by uncertainty about a company's legal position, rights, and obligations. Most privately owned firms address this problem by implementing strict cultural and behavioural rules. They say things like "ethical standards in our company surpass regulatory requirements." We don't want to look "clever" or push the boundaries of acceptable conduct.

• Reputational danger When your company's image suffers among the various groups of individuals who have a vested interest in its success, you endanger your own. Businesses that give advice, for example, must be ready to assume responsibility for the accuracy of the advice they provide. As the litigiousness of the American model spreads north, your potential liability in this area may grow. Penny Shore, a Toronto-based publisher, remembers that a few years ago if a reader was unhappy with the advice offered in a book, they might send a negative letter. In today's world, the conclusion may just as well be a court battle. She warns that even if the lawsuit is dropped, the damage to your reputation may be severe. Private companies that actively manage their risk have a better understanding of their operations, including their weak points and the potential for development that present itself. Risk management and corporate governance are shifting their emphasis away from compliance and towards development and efficiency.

Common Mistakes by Entrepreneurs

Venture capitalists frequently report being taken aback by the number of potential investors who are unaware of the errors that can sway their choice of whether to invest.

Lack of Personal Risk

If you do not invest any of your own money in your company, you cannot expect other people to do so either. You need to have "skin in the game" or investors will get the impression that you could bail out when things get difficult and grab a job at Google instead, which will happen anyway.

Poor Presentation of Financial Information

According to Mark McQueen, who works at Wellington Financial, "Another significant mistake" is passing out a spreadsheet that includes a listing of every item, including paper and envelopes. It is not necessary for you to disclose that information to the investors. You can make your details available to them if they want, but they do not need to examine every line of the profit and loss statement. If you do that, they might end up hitting their heads against the table. In addition, investors will want to receive their information on a quarterly basis, regardless of when your fiscal year ends; therefore, you should provide it to them using the standard tax calendar.

Not Knowing the Fund

You are not the only one attempting to "spin" the situation. The venture capitalists spin just as much, and they want you to take a significant risk on them just as much. It is a well-kept secret that fund managers and venture capitalists aspire to be well-known and admired as well. It implies that you are really enthused about them becoming a part of the team if you go into the trouble of researching them first. You should know by now that there are as many diverse types of funds as there are animals in a zoo; Google the funds, and read the information provided on their websites in detail. There is going to be a list of the companies that they have in their fund portfolio and looking at that list will make it abundantly evident which sectors of the economy they favor. At present point, there are funds available for any kind of business, ranging from mining and manufacturing to technology; nevertheless, you will need to familiarize yourself with their investment criteria. Visit the website of the CVCA to obtain contact information for a considerable number of private equity investors in Canada. Keep in mind that your sector has a need for people with their skills. Carry out some study. Who have they invested in before, and what do you have in common with the firms that they have supported in the past?

• Find out from the other business owners who are running companies in the portfolio what their venture capitalist has been doing for them recently.

• Is this fund willing to wait? You want to feel certain that they are not going to undertake a superficial review of your company but that they are interested in your long-term goals for the company.

• Will there still be money in the fund for the subsequent round of funding?

• Do they have a wide-ranging network of professional connections?

• What is the VC's track record in the industry? When you go for your next round of money (as your business grows), the subsequent investors will want to know who invested in the company the first time. If your investors have their headquarters in Las Vegas and look like characters from The Sopranos, you should pass on this opportunity. Know that this shortcut will one day be brought out into the harsh light of day, and it may cost you blue chip funding years down the road if you choose to take the easy route and get your business financed by some heavy in the "waste disposal" business who wears big knuckle rings. If you take this easy route, know that this shortcut will one day be brought out into the harsh light of day.

Lack of Standing in the Community

You will only contact a tiny number of private investors, and what you are selling is quite expensive. Assume you are your own investor. What would you do in this situation? This person is putting up between $1 million and $5 million of his own money in your firm. Is he going to give his money to someone who calls him and says, "Hey Joe, I hear you've got some extra money lying about, and I've got a terrific business for you?" In a million years, never. The investment community works in the same way as the six-degrees-of-separation concept, and its members will learn all they can about you. Jan Carlzon, the CEO of a bankrupt Scandinavian airline, was able to bring the firm back by instilling in his staff that the customer experience is a collaborative endeavor in which everyone participates. Each of these tiny things symbolizes a key moment: a time when the brand is reinforced when passengers are welcomed with a smile at the check-in counter, when they are placed on a pristine seat, and when they reach for a clean blanket. Consider the possibility that the bathroom was unclean. This pivotal moment would dampen the generally gratifying components of the customer's interaction. Clients may get the idea that the aircraft's upkeep is shoddy, leading them to conclude that the rest of the corporation, as demonstrated by the lavatory, is also negligent. Recruiting investors is about every interaction the investor has with you, from the first conversation to setting up the meeting to the paper you use for your investment proposal. It's all about making a statement about how you run your firm. Whether you start a blog or post on Facebook, keep in mind that your friends aren't the only ones who are reading your words of wisdom. Do not divulge information about your private equity partners "These VC jerks forced me to write a sixty-page plan that they didn't even read." Rick Segal of J.A. Albright, an evidently well-read venture capitalist, posted about this entrepreneur's blog gaffe on his blog! Be upfront if you have a strange cult in your history, such as a lawsuit. "Everyone lies," says Dr. House in the Emmy-winning TV series House. "Being a cynic and never trusting in anybody these last twenty years finally paid off," said a fund manager who had just received the top businessperson of the year award. A monkey can perform a superficial background check on Google, and fund managers have attorneys conduct more thorough checks. "A good reputation is more desirable than money," stated Pubulus Syros in 110 B.C.

A Word for Women

It has been stated that limited access to "old boy" networks and a male-dominated fi noncoal business has caused hurdles for women seeking expansion financing. "Th use conditions largely explain why women get just 6% of the $69B in venture capital available in the U.S.," says Ilse Treurnicht. "Still, women do not make it easy on themselves, either. A passive approach, restrictive mindset, and inability to 'talk the language' are only some of the things holding women back." The good news: attitudes are steadily improving and there is money available for quality, high-growth firms that can appropriately communicate their promise to investors. If you are female, build some thick skin and deal with the stereotypes early on in your talks. Here are a few: Why Woman entrepreneurs do not wish to build their firm as quickly as males do.

• Female entrepreneurs just do not "get" how to obtain funding.

• Lack of networks is one cause for women's issues. When women were asked about their networks, they listed various men's names. When those guys were asked about their networks, they did not mention the women. Before you write to your local newspaper to complain, take a breath. What is real are the data on male- vs female-run businesses which indicate that female enterprises may develop at a slower speed, but they tend to have a greater survival rate. Understand that, when it comes to obtaining private equity, fund managers favor the growth versus survival element. It is only logical that when you go about raising funds, your pitch must be on growing the business; otherwise, leave private equity to the more aggressive CEOs. Barbara Order, professor at Carlton University, reiterates that crucial point, "Here's the bottom line for women: only entrepreneurs who launch solid, high-potential businesses and express that promise will acquire the money they need." Smart women comprehend such thinking and reassure investors by spending more time displaying their ambition while reaching out to the VCs.

Do Your Homework

The words "Know Thyself" were first written down by the Scribes of Delphi and later by Plato. This ancient knowledge is still relevant today when it comes to getting to know the stakeholders of private equity, which are venture capitalists.

Markus Loft, a serial high-tech entrepreneur who is now an executive-in-residence expert for his former financial partners, Rayna, and who assists with the management of their portfolio of companies, offers the following piece of advice to aspiring business owners: "Entrepreneurs must know what their limitations are." According to Markus, business owners "must come to terms with their weaknesses and recognize what it is that they don't know." When every significant choice must be run by you first, you know it is time to start recruiting potential managers for your company. According to him, "If owners do not establish teams, they will find themselves out on the road selling while still being needed back at the office." There is a significant obstacle that is preventing expansion." Markus is an expert on the subject because he began his career as an entrepreneur at the age of fifty. Together with Rayna, he successfully guided two businesses down a road of expansion before selling them.

When I finally decided to sell Headwater in September of this past year, the company had eighty-five employees and had generated

$11.5 million in revenue.

To advance the company, Loft proposes taking into consideration the questions that are listed below.

• What differentiates you from other competitors?

• Where do you stand in the market?

When was the last time your business plan was updated?

• What kinds of cash flows are expected to be present?

• When do you plan to go public (if at all), and what is the strategy for getting there?

• What method will you use to construct your board? In what manner will it manage the company?

Who should be on the board, and what qualifications should they have?

• What is your plan for getting out of the business (multiples, EBITDA, or other sorts of valuation)?

You are required to be aware of the numerous factors at play and to understand each one. Markus cautions that "your value will be undermined" if you are unable to position your company effectively. Briefly, you should finish your assignments.

You Understand Controlled Greed

Someone with fundraising expertise cited Sophocles' words: "There is nothing in this world more discouraging than money." If venture investors reject your investment proposal, you should not take it personally. If you ask them what they think you should do or who else you should speak to, you could get some beneficial information.

Deal-making is something you will have no trouble with if you grasp the fear and greed that drive venture capitalists. Venture capitalists are not in the business of doing good. They are accountable for ensuring that their clients are pleased since it is their money. Dread, a far stronger emotion, lurks underneath what is often referred to as greed. Not only are VCs afraid of losing money on a transaction (you), but also of becoming the laughingstock of Wall Street, Bay Street, or Silicon Valley. Moreover, many are frightened of losing their savings and never being able to find work again. Their labor is done in the open. Private equity funding is not just the riskiest segment of the business world; it is also subject to intense scrutiny. If you believe what you learn in business textbooks, the risk should reduce as your firm grows, but it stays high for a much longer period. According to Rolf Fichus, who works with small and medium-sized firms (SMEs) at the National Research Council of Canada, when entrepreneurs participate in government initiatives, they seldom get the finance they needed or anticipated. Fichus works for a nonprofit that assists businesses. It's not a great deal, but you can purchase it for this price today only.

www.ingramcontent.com/pod-product-compliance
Lightning Source LLC
Chambersburg PA
CBHW071136220526
45467CB00015B/1232